domain.456

Substance Abuse
Communicating with Others
Who Is Jesus?

Bev Gundersen and Linda Kondracki

NEXGEN®

Building the New Generation of Believers

An Imprint of Cook Communications Ministries
COLORADO SPRINGS, COLORADO • PARIS, ONTARIO
KINGSWAY COMMUNICATIONS, LTD., EASTBOURNE, ENGLAND

NexGen® is an imprint of
Cook Communications Ministries, Colorado Springs, CO 80918
Cook Communications, Paris, Ontario
Kingsway Communications, Eastbourne, England

domain.456: Substance Abuse, Communicating with Others, Who Is Jesus?

© 1992, 2004 Cook Communications Ministries

First printing, 1992
First NexGen printing, 2004
Printed in United States of America
1 2 3 4 5 6 7 8 9 10 Printing/Year 08 07 06 05 04

Designed by Jeff Jansen
Illustrated by Sonny Carder

ISBN: 0-7814-5519-7

Table of Contents ✓

Welcome to the Junior Electives Series

 ## Let's talk about it . . .

What is it like to grow up in America today? How do our Junior-age children perceive the world around them, and their place in it? Did you know that your Junior students are more aware of the world around them than any previous generation of American children? However, seen through their eyes the world is often seen as a scary and anxious place. Every day they are blatantly confronted with the threat of nuclear disasters, ecological concerns that warn them their planet may not exist by the time they grow up, and an increasing number of their classmates either wielding knives and guns at school or killed in gang-related incidents. Closer to home, you can expect a high number of your students to have experienced at least one divorce in their family, or suffered some kind of physical, sexual, or emotional abuse from family members.

As adults, we may like to close our eyes and see the days of childhood as carefree and innocent as they might have been in our day. But when we open our eyes and see the world as our kids see it today, it is clear that life holds much stress and anxiety for our children. Instead of wishing for simpler days, it is time for us to say to our kids, "Let's talk about it . . ."

The Junior Electives Series was designed to help you do just that. Each topic in the series was selected because it represents issues Juniors are concerned about, and in many cases learning about from their peers, the media, or in school. With the help of this curriculum, you will be able to provide an opportunity for them to discuss their concerns in a Christian context. For many of your kids, this may be the first chance they will have to hear that the Bible has a lot to teach them about each of these contemporary life concerns.

As you teach the lessons in this series, you will have an opportunity to:

• Introduce and teach topics of concern to Juniors in a distinctively Christian context.

• Provide a safe place to learn about, talk about, and express feelings about each issue.

• Teach practical skills and biblical principles Juniors can use to cope with each concern in their daily lives.

• Provide a tool to help parents facilitate family discussion and coping in the home setting.

Features of the Junior Elective Series

Four-Part Lesson Plan

Each lesson follows this format:

1. Setting the Stage (5-10 minutes). Each lesson begins with an activity designed to do two things. First, it is a gathering activity, meaning that you can involve your students in it as soon as they arrive. You do *not* need to have the whole class present to begin your lesson time. By arriving early and having the Setting the Stage activity set up and ready for the kids as soon as they walk in the door, you will communicate a sense of excitement about the lesson and set a tone of orderliness for your class.

Secondly, the Setting the Stage activity is purposeful in that it will draw the students into the subject for the day. It is more than just something to keep the kids busy while everyone arrives. The activity will provide a fun and interesting way to draw the kids' attention to an area of interest in their lives. Most of the time, it will also raise questions which will lead them into the next section of the lesson.

2. Introducing the Issue (20 minutes). Building on the Setting the Stage activity, this section of the lesson will involve the kids in an active discussion of the topic of the day. The material provided for you contains information the kids need to know, anticipating key questions they may have. It also includes one or more learning activities particularly designed to encourage your students to talk about the issues most on their minds, while in the context of a Christian community. To make this time as effective as possible, you will need to establish your class as a safe place where everyone's feelings and questions are welcomed and treated seriously (some suggestions for doing that are listed on page 5). Once that has been accomplished, you may be surprised at how much your Juniors have to say, and the depth of their thinking!

3. Searching the Scriptures (20 minutes). This section of each lesson takes your class to the Bible to discover what God has to say about the topic being discussed. Your students may be amazed to find out just how much the Bible says about subjects that seem so *modern*. Through a wide variety of creative teaching methods, your class will study people and principles of Scripture that speak directly to the concerns gripping their hearts and minds. As you study together, you will also be acquainting them with the most valuable resource they can have for coping with these contemporary issues: their Bibles.

4. Living the Lesson (5-10 minutes). The final section of each lesson challenges the kids to take what they've learned and apply it to their own lives. It's the *so what* section. The class members will be encouraged to ask themselves, "So what am I going to do with what I've just learned?"

Clearly Stated Key Principles

Each book in the Junior Electives Series contains three units, each of which addresses a different topic of concern. The following three unit features will help your student focus on and remember the central principles of each unit.

1. Unit Verse. One verse has been chosen for each unit that summarizes the Biblical principle central to the unit topic. The meaning of this verse is developed a little more each week as students work on a cooperative learning activity designed to help them understand and apply a key biblical principle.

2. Unit Affirmation. The primary learning objective for each unit has been phrased into an affirmation sentence that begins with "I can . . . " Discussing this affirmation each week will empower your students by letting them know they can do something positive about issues that may feel frightening or overwhelming.

3. Unit Service Projects. At the end of each unit you will find several ideas for your class to not only learn about the unit issue, but actually DO something about it. Although they are optional, taking the extra time to involve your class in a unit project will help them practice new skills and see for themselves that they can take an active role in the issues that affect their lives.

Parent Informational Letter

At the beginning of each unit, you will find PARTNERS . . ., a newsletter which you can photocopy and send home to the parents of your class members. This letter gives parents an overview of the topic being studied, as well as some practical ideas of ways they can further their child's learning through several Do-At-Home activities.

Flexibility and Variety

The Junior Electives Series has been designed to be usable in any number of settings. It is equally effective in a Sunday school setting, a Wednesday night series, or even a special setting such as a weekend retreat. If you live in an area that participates in release time, this series is an exellent resource to present biblical principles in a contemporary way. Feel free to be creative and find the best place for your group to talk about these important life principles.

A variety of learning activities are used to present the issue information and biblical truths. The following materials are considered standard supplies and are recommended to be available for the classtimes:

- Bibles
- Glue
- Tape
- Pencils
- Scissiors
- Stapler
- Paper

A Word About Children and Stress . . .

As you prepare to teach the Junior Electives Series, it is important to realize that many of the subjects you will be studying are the sources of stress in the lives of your students. Many students may never have had the chance to talk openly about these issues, and doing so in your class may well raise their anxiety level. Throughout these sessions, there are several things you can keep in mind:

1) Point them to Jesus. Perhaps the greatest benefit of the Junior Electives Series is that it will give you the opportunity to help your kids learn that a relationship to Jesus Christ is the best resource we can have to face the stressful, anxious parts of our lives. Through the Bible studies and your own personal witness of the power of Christ in your life, you can have the privilege of introducing children to Jesus and inviting them to ask Him to be an active part of their lives.

2) Create a safe place where they can talk about their real feelings. Children have a strong tendency to say the things in class that they think teachers want to hear. Early on in this series, you will want to create a safe place for sharing by continually reassuring your kids that they can say what is really on their minds, and making a rule that no one can criticize or make fun of anything anyone else shares in class. In many cases, expressing their feelings in a safe place, and having those feelings accepted by you and the class will relieve much of their anxiety.

3) If necessary, help them get outside help. You may find a child in your class who is experienceing an unusual amount of stress. In that case, ask your pastor or Christian Education Director for the procedure your church uses to refer children and families for professional help.

Drug Wars . . .

Statistics concerning children and drug use are sobering. A survey taken by the National Parents Resource Institute for Drug Education reports that 100,000 Junior-age children said they get drunk at least once a week, and another 185,000 sixth graders alone had used hard liquor at some time. From the American Guidance Service we learn that the percentage of children using drugs by sixth grade tripled between 1975 and 1987!

The need to educate our children concerning drug abuse *before* they are confronted with alcohol and other drugs has been proclaimed widely throughout our nation. Your students have probably already participated in excellent drug prevention programs in their schools or other community settings. They may have also seen media coverage aimed at getting through to kids concerning the dangers of abusing chemicals. However, many of your Juniors have most likely never discussed the issue in a distinctly Christian environment. Therefore, during this unit you will have an opportunity to help your kids on two levels. First, you will cover the basics by giving them good information about why and how to avoid drug use. But more importantly, you will take them to Scripture to learn how their relationship to God and the principles of the Bible can give them all the resources and power they need to say NO to drugs!

✓ Substance Abuse Overview

Unit Verse: My God will meet all your needs according to his glorious riches in Christ Jesus. Philippians 4:19
Unit Affirmation: I CAN SAY NO TO DRUGS!

LESSON	TITLE	OBJECTIVE	SCRIPTURE BASE
Lesson #1	How Do Drugs Affect My Body?	That your students will regard their bodies as temples of God and not abuse them with harmful substances.	II Corinthians 6:16–7:1
Lesson #2	Why Do People Take Drugs?	That your students will turn to God to help them during times of stress or when they have low self-esteem.	Judges 6:11-16; 7:1-25
Lesson #3	Read My Lips—No Drugs!	That your students will use God's power to help them refuse harmful substances.	Daniel 1:1-20
Lesson #4	Family Matters	That your students will seek God's comfort and power in families where there is substance abuse.	II Timothy 2:22-26
Lesson #5	How Can I Help You?	That your students will have the desire to reach out in God's love to help their friends who abuse substances.	Titus 2:11–3:8

Partners

For the next few weeks your Junior-age child will be part of a group learning about Substance Abuse. *Partners* is a planned parent piece to keep you informed of what will be taught during this exciting series.

PREVIEW...
Substance Abuse

Every parent worries about kids and drugs, and with good reason. Statistics concerning children and drug use are sobering. A survey taken by the National Parents Resource Institute for Drug Education reports that 100,000 ten-and eleven-year-old children said they get drunk at least once a week, and another 185,000 sixth graders alone had used hard liquor at some time. From the American Guidance Service we learn that the percentage of children using drugs by sixth grade tripled between 1975 and 1987!

As the age our children experiment with drugs gets lower, the need to educate them concerning drug abuse *before* they are confronted with alcohol and other drugs increases. In recent years, this need has been proclaimed widely throughout our nation. Your kids may have already participated in excellent drug prevention programs in their schools or other community settings. However, unless you have talked with them at home, this unit may be the first time they have discussed the issue from a Christian viewpoint. The next few weeks will be helpful to your kids on two levels. First, they will receive good information about why and how to avoid drug use. But more importantly, they will learn from Scripture how their relationship to God and the principles of the Bible can give them all the resources and power they need to say NO to drugs!

Unit Verse:

My God will meet all your needs according to his glorious riches in Christ Jesus. Philippians 4:19

Unit Affirmation:

I CAN SAY NO TO DRUGS!

PRINCIPLES...
Substance Abuse

PRINCIPLE #1:

THE FIRST STEP IN PREVENTING DRUG ABUSE IS KNOWING THE USES AND ABUSES OF THE COMMON DRUGS USED BY CHILDREN.

MARIJUANA is the second most common drug used by children. Effects include a sense of well being, a state of relaxation, and altered perceptions. The greatest danger is leading to experimentation with more dangerous drugs, and developing a psychological dependence on the false sense of feeling good it produces.

STIMULANTS are used to increase mental activity and offset drowsiness. Amphetamines are stimulants used as diet pills and as an antidote to mild depression. Cocaine is the most dangerous stimulant, and "crack", a form of cocaine, is considered highly dangerous. All stimulants are physically addictive.

DEPRESSANTS are the opposite of stimulants, and include barbiturates, tranquilizers and alcohol. They are often prescribed by doctors to relieve pain and anxiety and bring sleep. Alcohol is the most common drug used by children. It is easily accessible, socially acceptable and not considered dangerous by many. All of the depressants are physically addictive.

INHALANTS are household substances that produce intoxicating fumes. Because they are so easy to obtain, many kids begin experimenting with chemicals by placing these substances in a plastic bag and inhaling the fumes. The high can last a few minutes or hours and the effects are very dangerous.

NARCOTICS are often prescribed by doctors to reduce pain, relieve tension, bring sleep and slow breathing and pulse rate. The major narcotics, including codeine, morphine, opium, heroin and methadone are very important in medicine when used under a doctor's supervision. They are, however, very addictive even when used for only a short time.

PRINCIPLE #2:

THE SECOND STEP IN PREVENTING DRUG ABUSE IS KNOWING THE REASONS WHY KIDS TAKE DRUGS. A 1987 Weekly Reader survey of fourth through sixth graders cited these reasons for children taking drugs :
• Television and movies make drugs seem attractive.
• Influence of other children–the need to "fit in".
• To have a good time.
• To feel older.
In spite of the efforts of so many people working in drug prevention programs, many thousands of children will give in to peer pressure and get

hooked on chemicals every year. The reality is that kids get drugs from other kids. Helping our kids deal with peer pressure is one of the most important preventive steps we can take.

PRINCIPLE #3:

THE THIRD STEP OF PREVENTING DRUG ABUSE IS KNOWING THE SIGNS OF ABUSE IN CHILDREN. There are many signs that point to potential drug abuse. These signs may be subtle at first, and become more pronounced as the abuse increases. Parents must be alert and ready to take action if they notice one or more of these signs developing in their child:
• Any drastic change in normal behavior (eating, sleeping, interaction with others) or appearance
• Increased need for money
• Extreme changes in moods and emotional tone
• New friends who are known drug users; loss of interest in old friends
• Loss of interest in physical and extracurricular activities
• Secret behaviors concerning friends, activities, or phone calls
• Extreme withdrawal
• Wearing sun glasses to hide eyes

PREVENTION...
Substance Abuse
1. HIDE GOD'S WORD IN YOUR HEART.

As a family, memorize the Unit Verse, Philippians 4:19 as a constant reminder of God's invitation to trust Him, not drugs, with all that we need. Memorizing I Corinthians 6:19, 20 is also a good idea. These verses remind kids that their bodies are God's temple, and we are responsible to care for them well!

2. GIVE YOUR CHILDREN A DRUG-FREE COMMUNITY IN WHICH TO GROW UP.

Peer pressure and modeling are the two greatest contributing factors to children getting involved with drugs. Be sure your family has a strong connection with other families that share your values concerning chemical use. Kids need the influence of adults outside the family to reinforce the values you are teaching, as well as a solid base of kids who you also know well. If you do not have a number of other families that your family interacts with regularly, take steps to build this kind of community for your kids *and* you. Spend time *often* doing fun things together, including providing lots of time to talk with and listen to the kids. It will meet the needs of belonging and excitement that kids often look to the drug community to find.

How Do Drugs Affect My Body?

Aim: That your students will regard their bodies as temples of God and not abuse them with harmful substances.

Scripture: II Corinthians 6:16-7:1

Unit Verse: My God will meet all your needs according to his glorious riches in Christ Jesus. Philippians 4:19

Unit Affirmation: I CAN SAY NO TO DRUGS!

✓ Planning Ahead

1. Photocopy activity sheets (pages 15 and 16)–one for each student.
2. Prepare the following materials for SETTING THE STAGE:
   Draw a large target on a poster board, leaving the center bull's-eye blank. Cut circles the size of the bull's-eye out of black paper–one for each student. On an 8 1/2" x 11" piece of paper, write the words: "She sells seashells by the seashore."
3. Set up activity stations for SETTING THE STAGE
4. Prepare the Unit Affirmation poster by writing across the top of a large poster board the words: "I CAN SAY NO TO DRUGS". Under the title, write the numbers 1-5 vertically down the left-hand side.
5. Make a bottle visual as described in SEARCHING THE SCRIPTURES.
6. Make a heart visual as described in SEARCHING THE SCRIPTURES.
7. Prepare the Unit Verse add-on banner. Cut six 12" burlap squares. Use a zig-zag stitch to sew an edging, or apply a coat of white craft glue around all block edges to prevent fraying.
8. Print the Unit Verse on one block using a fine-tip, permanent-ink felt marker. Weekly blocks will be sewn to this verse square as lessons progress.

1 Setting the Stage (5-10 minutes)

WHAT YOU'LL DO

- Participate in three activities to simulate the effects of drugs on normal functioning

WHAT YOU'LL NEED

- Materials for "Pin the bull's-eye to the target"
- "She sells seashells by the seashore" sign
- A blindfold, a stand up mirror, black construction paper

2 Introducing the Issue (20 minutes)

WHAT YOU'LL DO

- Use an activity sheet to study the uses and abuses of various drugs
- Introduce the Unit Affirmation poster and add a phrase to the first line

WHAT YOU'LL NEED

- "Caution: Chemicals at Work!" Activity Sheet (page 15)
- Unit Affirmation poster

3 Searching the Scriptures (20 minutes)

WHAT YOU'LL DO

- Recognize that God regards their bodies as His holy dwelling place
- See object lessons which show the results of using their bodies for drugs contrasted with using them as God's temple

WHAT YOU'LL NEED

- Bibles
- Bottle and heart visuals

4 Living the Lesson (5-10 minutes)

WHAT YOU'LL DO

- Use an activity sheet to determine ways substances are being used wisely or abused
- Make a block for the add-on banner

WHAT YOU'LL NEED

- "Gumming Up The Works?" Activity Sheet (page 16)
- Unit Verse burlap square
- One 12" burlap squares, felt, scissors, white craft glue, markers
- Optional: bubblegum - piece for each student

Setting the Stage (5-10 minutes)

Before your students arrive today, set up three activity stations around the room.

1. PIN THE BULL'S-EYE TO THE TARGET. Attach the target to the wall. (See PLANNING AHEAD.) Have available a blindfold, one bull's-eye for each student, and tape. Instructions: Working with a partner, stand six feet from the target. Blindfold your partner and give him or her a bull's-eye with a roll of tape on the back. Turn him or her around three times, then encourage your partner to stick the bull's-eye onto the target.

2. TONGUE TWISTER. On a table place the paper with the words: "She sells seashells by the seashore" and a cassette player with a cassette tape. Instructions: Take turns saying this tongue twister five times quickly into the cassette player.

3. MIRROR, MIRROR. Place a small stand-up mirror, a piece of black construction paper and blank paper and pencils in this center. Instructions: One person sits at the table with a piece of paper in front of him or her, and the mirror standing in back of the paper so you can see the reflection of the paper in the mirror. Your partner will then hold the piece of construction paper in front of you so that the only thing you can see is the reflection of the paper and pencil in the mirror. Now draw a five pointed star by looking in the mirror. If you have time, write your name the same way. Switch places.

As the kids arrive, place them in pairs and instruct them to visit all three centers. When all have had a chance to try the activities, gather everyone together again. **Did you have any trouble doing any of the activities? How did it feel to lose your normal perceptions by being blindfolded and looking in a mirror?** Let kids respond. **Today we are starting a new unit about drugs. We'll begin by talking about the effects of drugs on our bodies. Like the games we just played, drugs interfere with our ability to control what we are doing. Also like our games, some kids think that is fun. Today we will see the difference between playing games and abusing drugs!**

Introducing the Issue (20 minutes)

Since many schools and communities are now offering extensive drug awareness programs, begin this session by letting the kids share with you what they already know about drugs. **How many of you have studied drug abuse** in school or other settings? **What are the things you remember most from what you've already learned?** Give the kids several minutes to tell you what they already know. **Why do you think so many people are working so hard to warn you about drugs?** It is normal for Juniors to feel "it will never happen to me" about many things, including the dangers of using drugs. With so many opportunities around, each of your kids *will* be confronted with alcohol and/or other drug use very soon, if not already. The best protection they can have is good information and constant reminders about the dangers of experimentation and use.

Distribute copies of the activity sheet "Caution: Chemicals at Work!" (page 15). Work together to fill in the chart, using the following information.

MARIJUANA is the second most common drug used by children. The effects include a sense of well being, a state of relaxation, and altered perceptions. Since it produces a pleasant effect and in many circles is not considered addictive, marijuana is readily available on school campuses. The greatest danger is that it can lead to experimentation with more dangerous drugs, and the development of a psychological dependence on the false sense of feeling good it produces.

STIMULANTS are used to increase mental activity and offset drowsiness. Many students use stimulants to put in long hours of studying. They are also used as diet pills and as an antidote to mild depression. Cocaine is the most dangerous stimulant, and "crack," a form of cocaine is considered highly dangerous. All stimulants are physically addictive.

DEPRESSANTS are the opposite of stimulants. They are often prescribed by doctors to relieve pain and anxiety and bring sleep. Because of their calming effect, they are a desirable drug for anyone feeling particularly tense. Alcohol, which is a depressant, is the most common drug used by children. It is easily accessible, socially acceptable and not considered dangerous by many. All of the depressants are physically addictive.

INHALANTS are household substances that produce intoxicating fumes. Because they are so easy to obtain, many kids begin experimenting with chemicals. The high can last a few minutes or hours and the effects are very dangerous. There are *no* good reasons to do this!

NARCOTICS are often prescribed by doctors to reduce pain, relieve tension, bring sleep and slow breathing and pulse rate. They are very important in medicine, when used under a doctor's supervision. They are, however, very addictive even when used for only a short time.

From our discussion, what do you think is the difference between drug USE and drug ABUSE? Let kids respond before filling in these blanks on their activity sheets. Point out that used properly and under medical supervi-

sion, drugs can be a help in our lives. However, when we begin taking drugs for fun or because we have to have them to feel good, we are abusing them. It's like having a stove. Used properly, it is a good thing to have in our lives. However, if we insist on putting our hand on the burner and keeping it there, we will get burned!

Display the Unit Affirmation poster and ask the class to read it aloud together. Then write the phrase, ". . . because they CAN hurt me" on the first line. **Don't be a "It will Never Happen To Me!" kid. If you play with drugs,** *you will get hurt by them.* **Now let's take a look at what the Bible has to say about drug use.**

☑ Searching the Scriptures (20 minutes)

Have available these object lessons you have made before class.

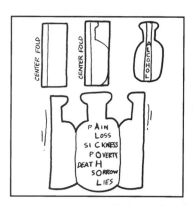

Bottle Visual: Fold a piece of tan paper 8 1/2" x 11" in the middle so it measures 4 1/4" x 11". Fold each long edge to within 1/4" of the center fold so it now measures 2 1/8" x 11". With the center fold on your left, cut a shape like half a bottle. In the opening between the flaps print the word "ALCOHOL" vertically in bold letters. Open the flaps and using these letters, complete an acrostic with these words: PAIN, LOSS, SICKNESS, POVERTY, DEATH, SORROW.

Heart Visual: Fold a red piece of paper 8 1/2" x 11" crosswise so it measures 5 1/2" x 8 1/2", then 2 7/8" x 8 1/2". With the center fold on your left, cut a shape like half a heart. This will be a rather elongated shape and can be shortened if preferred. In the opening between the flaps print the word "TEMPLE" vertically in bold letters. Open the flaps and using these letters, complete an acrostic with the words: STRENGTH, PEACE, PROMISES, HOPE, LIFE, LOVE.

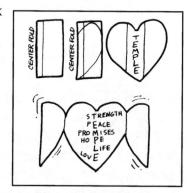

Does the Bible have anything to say about our bodies and drugs? Let's turn to II Corinthians 6:16-7:1 and find out. Ask several volunteers to take turns reading this passage. Pass out paper and have students work in pairs listing all the basic facts of these verses. Discuss their findings as a group. The

facts mentioned are: we (our bodies) are the temple of the living God, God lives in us, we are to keep away from unclean (harmful) things, we should turn away from things that are wrong and stay free from anything that makes our bodies or spirits unclean, use our bodies for God alone.

From these facts, why is it important that we not abuse our bodies with harmful substances? (Because God regards our bodies as His holy dwelling place, His temple.) **How do you feel about having God live in your body?** (Awed, thrilled, surprised, excited.) **The Bible doesn't use the word "drugs" specifically, but it does talk about unclean things that can spoil our bodies. One of these harmful substances is alcohol.** Show bottle visual and talk about its appeal to some people. **Let's see what happens when we abuse this substance.** Open the flaps. **What does it bring us?** (Pain, loss, sickness, poverty, death, sorrow, lies.) **All these things are like garbage that spoils our bodies and our lives**.

Show heart visual. **We'll let this heart symbolize our body as God's temple.** Open the flaps. **What does God bring us when we keep our bodies free from wrong things?** (Strength, peace, promises, hope, life, love.) **Which things would you rather have?** (The things God brings.) **Look back into the Bible passage we read earlier. What promise does God give us if we stay free from things that make our bodies unclean?** (He promises to be a Father to us.) **How does the prospect of being a child of the All-Powerful God make you feel?** (Great, excited, like I don't want to "blow" it by getting hooked on drugs.)

We've said that there is a difference between proper use and misuse of drugs. But you need to be able to judge if they are being used wisely or abused. Distribute copies of the activity sheet "Gumming up the Works?" (page 16).

Explain that you want the kids to make responses whenever you get to special words printed bold in the story. Sounds: BUBBLEGUM—chomp, chomp, chomp; FRIENDS—Hi there; JAWS—watch out!; ANTI—No, No! Practice these responses with the kids just to get them warmed up. If you feel it is helpful, write the words and their responses on the board. Read the story, pausing for each response.

Have kids mark their decisions on the activity sheet. Because the enjoyment of this activity may detract from the serious subject it presents, you may want to have students read back over the story silently before marking their choices. Discuss the results as a group.

What signs in the story did you find that helped you determine if the gum was abused? (Sore jaws; gum in hair, under chairs, in dishwater, stuck to the cat; skipping school; sneaking it into lockers and desks; accidents with

their bikes.) Stress the fact that the substance itself wasn't the problem. **What was the real problem here?** (The attitude of the kids and their use of the gum.)

How did others take advantage of this addiction to bubble gum? (They overcharged and cheated each other.) **Does that kind of thing happen when people abuse drugs?** Explain your answer. Many times drugs are offered as "free" gifts to first-time users. The object is to get people hooked on these destructive substances so they will have to keep buying them. As the body craves more drugs, addicts often find the price goes up. In the end they are willing to sell or steal anything they can to satisfy their desires for these devastating substances. The final result is often either death by overdose or murder by others who are as desperate as the addicts themselves.

Ask a volunteer to read Philippians 4:19. **Does this verse mean that God will give you drugs or money to buy them if you become addicted to harmful substances?** (No.) **Is there a difference between things you want and things you need?** Explain. Let students discuss this in relationship to their own lives. That means the necessities of life like food, clothing, shelter, versus the perks like VCRs, boom boxes, jewelry, bikes, designer clothes, sports equipment, etc.

We might paraphrase this verse by saying: God protect you from the harmful effects of drugs if you will keep away from anything that spoils your body, His house.

Living the Lesson (5-10 minutes)

Display the burlap square with the Unit Verse on it. Explain that students will make an add-on banner with squares illustrating this verse. Each week of this unit the class will make another block to be attached to this Unit Verse Block.

Decide as a group what truth about substance abuse you want to portray from today's lesson. Choose a brief slogan such as "No abuse—temple in use." Then divide up the work. Pass out the felt, markers, and scissors and let half the class make the slogan. The other half can cut symbols that illustrate it. Glue the slogan and symbols on the blank burlap square.

Having God live in your body is an awesome experience. Ask volunteers to close in prayer thanking God for living in their bodies and asking Him to help them take good care of these special temples.

OPTIONAL: Give a piece of bubble gum to each kid and as they chew it ask them to remember their bodies are God's dwelling place.

CAUTION: Chemicals At Work! ✓

We put chemicals into our bodies for many reasons. Many of the reasons are good ones. There is a big difference between USING drugs wisely and ABUSING them. Knowing the difference can be a life saver!

Substance	Where do you get it/them?	What are the effects?	What are the dangers?
MARIJUANA			
STIMULANTS: Amphetamines, cocaine, Crack, caffeine			
DEPRESSANTS: Barbiturates, tranquilizers, alcohol			
INHALANTS: nail polish remover, paints, airplane glue, gasoline			
NARCOTICS: codeine, morphine, opium, heroin, methadone			

Drug **USE** is _____

Drug **ABUSE** is _____

Activity Sheet by Linda Kondracki © 1991 David C. Cook Publishing Co. Permission granted to reproduce for classroom use only.

Gumming Up the Works?

In a state near you there are some kids who have a strange social activity that has affected their whole town. One day a boy found a sticky substance that tasted good and was fun to chew. He experimented a little and found he could blow bubbles with it. He hurried off to show all his **friends** his new discovery. They asked him what he called the material. Because his mouth was very full when he spoke, the answer came out "Bbbllummm." From then on the substance came to be called **bubble gum.**

The boy discovered something interesting about the **bubble gum.** When he felt angry or stressed out, chewing the bubble gum very hard made him feel better. The boy told the other kids this and everyone immediately wanted to try it. Before long the chewing and bubble blowing increased and the town became divided into four groups: The "**Jaws Bubble gum** Chewers," the "**Casual Bubble** gum Chewers," the "**Gourmet Bubble gum** Chewers" and the "**Anti-Bubble gum** Chewers."

The **Jaws Bubble gum** Chewers developed strong **jaws** and lungs and got together every week to blow lots of bubbles. They did it to relax after a stressful week or to be with their **friends.** Some felt worthless and thought this showed they were important. Each kid felt his or her reason for chewing **bubble gum** was worth it, even though they often had sore **jaws** and sticky faces the next day and promised themselves never to chew **bubble gum** again.

The Casual **Bubble gum** chewers chewed **bubble gum** every once in a while. When they joined the "**Jaws**" group, they usually blew only one medium-sized bubble. These kids chewed **bubble gum** for all the same reasons as the "**Jaws**" group, but were careful to miss the after-effects of the next day.

The Gourmet chewers turned **bubble gum** into a craft. They improved the regular **bubble gum** and even made their own. And wonderful Gourmet **bubble gum** they made too! They sold their products to the other kids, often overcharged them and even cheated each other.

Then there were the "**Anti-Bubble Gum** Chewers." They had seen the problems arising from **bubble gum** and loudly opposed it saying everyone should be **ANTI bubble gum!** Some of these **ANTIs** said that **bubble gum** caused **friends** to fight and break up friendships. Many kids had arguments with their parents who complained of **bubble gum** in hair, under chairs, in the dishwater, and even stuck to the family cat. Several **friends** skipped school to chew **bubble gum** or sneaked it into their lockers and desks so they could chew it at recess and in rest rooms. Some "**Jaws**" had even gotten so involved in blowing bubbles that they didn't pay attention and rode their bikes into trees and pedestrians, hurting themselves and others.

With all the problems and discussions going on, the **bubble gum** issue became a serious matter. Some kids absolutely wouldn't chew **bubble gum** while others couldn't face life without it. The time had come for every kid to make up his or her own mind.

What would you decide about the bubble gum? Put a check mark by your decision and be prepared to give reasons why you made it.

_____: Chewing bubble gum is OK and you can get sore jaws if you like.
_____: Casual bubble gum chewing is OK but it's wrong to get stuck in it.
_____: Chewing bubble gum is wrong at all times.

Lesson 2 ✔

Why Do People Take Drugs?

Aim: That your students will turn to God to help them during times of stress or when they have low self-esteem.

Scripture: Judges 6:11-16, 7:1-25

Unit Verse: My God will meet all your needs according to his glorious riches in Christ Jesus. Philippians 4:19

Unit Affirmation: I CAN SAY NO TO DRUGS!

 Planning Ahead

1. Photocopy activity sheets (pages 23 and 24)–one for each student.
2. Prepare three poster boards as Graffiti Boards for SETTING THE STAGE by writing one of these questions in the middle of each board: "What are ways we can handle bad feelings?" "What are some things we do to be accepted by our friends?" "What are things we do for excitement and to experience new things?" Hang the Graffiti Boards in three different areas of your classroom.
3. Attach by sewing or gluing last week's Unit Verse square to Bible verse block of add-on banner.
4. Make mini-Popsicles as described in SEARCHING THE SCRIPTURES.
5. Make a Mobius strip as described in SEARCHING THE SCRIPTURES.

1 Setting the Stage (5-10 minutes)

WHAT YOU'LL DO

- Write phrases on Graffiti Boards to introduce reasons why people take drugs

WHAT YOU'LL NEED

- Graffiti Boards

2 Introducing the Issue (20 minutes)

WHAT YOU'LL DO

- Discuss three needs people have that lead them to take drugs
- Use an activity sheet to see that taking drugs is a CHOICE we make
- Add a phrase to the Unit Affirmation poster

WHAT YOU'LL NEED

- Graffiti Boards from SETTING THE STAGE
- "The Choice is Mine!" Activity Sheet (page 23)
- Unit Affirmation poster

3 Searching the Scriptures (20 minutes)

WHAT YOU'LL DO

- Take part in activities which portray the various effects of drugs
- Use an activity sheet to read a skit to see how God can help with problems that cause substance abuse

WHAT YOU'LL NEED

- Bibles
- Mini-Popsicles
- Mobius strip
- "I'll See It When I Believe It!" Activity Sheet (page 24)

4 Living the Lesson (5-10 minutes)

WHAT YOU'LL DO

- Explore alternatives to using drugs
- Make a block for the add-on banner

WHAT YOU'LL NEED

- One 12" burlap square, felt, scissors, white craft glue, markers

 Setting the Stage (5-10 minutes)

As students arrive, instruct them to visit each Graffiti Board and read the question in the center of each one. (See PLANNING AHEAD.) Encourage them to write their answers in the space around the question. They can visit each Board more than once, since reading the answers of others can spark new answers they hadn't thought of before. As they work, circulate among them making suggestions if they need help. After a few minutes, call time and gather the class together.

Did anyone think to put "take drugs" on any of the Graffiti Boards? Let kids respond. Some may have thought of it, but didn't write it down. Others may have put it on first just because this is a unit on drugs. **These Graffiti Boards will help us take a look at our subject for today: reasons why people take drugs.**

✓ Introducing the Issue (20 minutes)

Before beginning the following discussion, reposition the Graffiti Boards, if necessary, so that everyone can read them easily. **If using chemicals is as bad as so many people say they are, why does anyone use them at all?** Let kids share their ideas. **There are basically three reasons why kids (or anyone) gets involved with drugs. They are represented on our Graffiti Boards. Let's take a look at them one at a time.**

Begin with the first Board and read the question in the middle, **"What are ways we can handle bad feelings?" No one likes to feel bad feelings. What are some feelings we don't like to feel?** (Possible responses include sadness, anger, rejection, feeling left out, failure, etc.) Help the kids generate a long list of these. **What are the things we do to cover up bad feelings?** Review the answers on the Graffiti Board. **Can you think of more things other than what is listed here?** (Possible responses include: going to my room, crying, praying, eating a whole package of Oreo cookies, drawing pictures, running around the block, hitting or hugging a pillow, talking to a friend, asking for a hug, etc.) **And, of course, using drugs and alcohol. In our country, people will go to great lengths to get rid of bad feelings. Unfortunately, the ways we choose aren't always healthy. Like drinking alcohol or taking drugs.**

Now look at the second Graffiti Board, and read the question on it, **"What are some things we do to be accepted by our friends?"** Everyone wants to belong to a group, or several groups. Belonging is a basic need of life. **What**

are some things we will do to feel accepted by others in groups we want to be a part of? Review the answers on the Graffiti Board. **Again, can you think of more things?** (Possibilities include: dress like they do, have a party and invite them to come, hang out with them, share secrets, follow the leader of the group, maybe steal or cheat if it is necessary to be accepted, and experiment with alcohol and other drugs if that is an important part of the group's activities.)

Sometimes our need for belonging is stronger than our desire to stand up for what we know or believe to be right. For some kids that means experimenting with alcohol and other drugs, even though they know it is a dumb thing to do. **Letting our belonging needs get in the way of our common sense is a dangerous thing to do.**

Go on to the third Graffiti Board and read the question, **"What are things we do for excitement and to experience new things?"** As human beings, we all have an inborn desire to experience new things and feel thrills and excitement. Life would be incredibly boring if we never took any risks. Review what was written on the board. **Are there any other exciting things you'd like to add to our list?** (Possibilities are endless, and will vary according to the interests of the individual. Just to mention a few: white water rafting, ballooning, skydiving, learning a new sport, skiing, competing in tournaments, etc.) **Risk taking can add enjoyment to our lives, *when* we carefully consider the risk involved. For instance, sky diving is an exciting activity, but as long as you follow the rules carefully, it is also a fairly safe activity. Jumping off a cliff with the hopes that you will fly is also an exciting activity. But the risk of seriously injuring yourself is extremely high! As we said last week, kids your age tend to think of themselves as totally indestructible; "It will never happen to ME!" When you believe that, experimenting with drugs and alcohol is just another exciting activity. But be warned! The risk of being seriously hurt by playing around with chemicals is *very high!***

When all is said and done, the main reason kids use drugs is because they *choose* to do so. No one makes them do it. Whatever the reason, every individual makes his or her own decision to get involved with chemical use. Distribute copies of the activity sheet, "The Choice is Mine" (page 23). Use the Graffiti Boards to complete the sheets. Review the choices you listed, asking kids to choose three positive ones to write next to the "Thumbs Up", and three negative choices to write next to the "Thumbs Down." Be sure the use of alcohol and other drugs are listed under each of the "Thumbs Down."

Display the Unit Affirmation poster and read the Affirmation aloud together.

Ask the class to think of a phrase they could write on the second line. A possibility is ". . . and YES to wiser, healthier choices." **Let's take a closer look at some of the choices, other than using chemicals, that are available to us.**

 # Searching the Scriptures (20 minutes)

Before class, make mini-Popsicles by freezing fruit juice in an ice cube tray. Before freezing them, cover the cubes with a plastic wrap and stick in toothpicks for handles. The wrap will hold the toothpicks upright until the cubes freeze. Make one Popsicle for each student.

Make a Mobius strip by cutting a 2" wide strip of newspaper. Turn one end of the strip over twice, then tape the ends together to form a loop. This kind of strip is a science oddity known as a Mobius strip.

Pass out the mini-Popsicles to students. Let kids eat them while you briefly review the reasons people take drugs. The Popsicles will quickly melt. **How long did the Popsicles last?** (Not very long; not long enough.) **Taking drugs to help you with your problems is like eating those Popsicles. The "high" you feel is very brief. At first a drug might make you feel good or make you forget your troubles, but those feelings soon go away. They are only a temporary "quick-fix." You find you have to take more and more drugs to get the same feeling and you soon have a worse problem than you did before.**

Ask for a volunteer. Slip the newspaper Mobius strip over his or her head. **Let's suppose that this piece of newspaper is a drug. You take it once or twice to help you face a problem. At first you think you can get rid of it easily. But if you keep on taking that drug, pretty soon it can become like a rope noose around your neck that can kill you. Because drugs cause chemical changes in your brain as well as your body, you begin to think you have to have them all the time. Before you realize it you're hooked. Now the drugs begin to run your life.**

This not only affects you, but everybody around you. Ask for three more volunteers. Remove the strip and cut the link down the center lengthwise. You now have two loops linked together. Divide each of these loops by

cutting lengthwise down the center of each strip. You will now have four loops all linked together. Slip one loop over the head of each of the four volunteers. **Soon you get other people involved in the same enslaving habit you have.** Remove the loops.

By now you may be thinking there has to be a better way to meet your needs, and there is. Let's see how somebody else did it without drugs.

Distribute copies of the activity sheet "I'll See It When I Believe It!," (page 24). Choose two of your better readers to take the parts of the interviewer and Gideon. The rest of the class can follow along on their handouts.

Discuss the skit comparing Gideon's problems and solutions with those of today's kids. **What personal problems did Gideon have?** (His family was unimportant, he felt worthless, he was afraid, his home and life were in danger from enemies.) **Many of these are the same problems Juniors face today. How did he feel about God?** (That God had left him or didn't care about him.) **How do you think Gideon might have coped with these problems?** Even though many of the drugs that we have today were not obtainable in Bible times, alcohol was readily available. Gideon would not have been the first or only person to turn to wine as an escape from his problems.

When the angel told Gideon God was with him and would help him face his problems how did Gideon react? (He was still hesitant and scared.) Point out that God didn't get upset or angry at his doubts, but continued to reassure Gideon of His help.

What happened to the enemy when Gideon trusted and obeyed God? (God made them kill each other in confusion and run away in fear, they were defeated.) **What do you think Gideon meant by "You'll see it when you believe it?"** Give kids some time to think and talk about this on their own before giving your input. It's the exact opposite of what society teaches them. But God's ways are not the ways of people. Over and over we find in the Bible this same clear-cut principle. We need to step out in faith that God will do something before we can actually see it.

 Living the Lesson (5-10 minutes)

Drugs are only a lie. They promise something great like courage, well-being,

feeling good. But it's all in your head. When you take drugs you lose the real "you." It's similar to wearing a mask all the time and not knowing what the person behind it is really like.

Suppose you are the parent of a child who is facing problems and thinking about taking drugs. What alternatives would you suggest to him or her? Have students help make a list of alternatives on the board. Kids could come up and write their suggestions. Some alternatives might be: talking problems over with drug-free family or friends; seeking help from a responsible adult you can trust like a school counselor, pastor, or teacher; make friends with kids who aren't druggies; find things that are fun to do and give you a natural high like joining a club or getting a new hobby; get some physical exercise to utilize your body's own euphoria-causing chemicals; use your imagination to take you on "trips" to great places or make up a story; take time to get to know the "real" you and the wonderful God who made you. If you love sports but know you can't make the team find something to do connected with athletics like being a team manager. You could even offer to be a sports photographer or reporter for your school paper.

Getting to know the real you is not an easy task. Recognizing your feelings, accepting and being able to share them with others can be a scary, risky thing. If you are reluctant to talk to people, talk to God. Have students read the Unit Verse (Philippians 4:19) from their Bibles. **How many needs does God promise to supply for us so we don't need to take drugs?** (All of them.) **God understands and cares about you more than anybody else does.**

Work on the next section of the Unit Verse add-on banner. Have kids decide how they can best illustrate the truth from today's lesson. Hand out felt, scissors, and markers. Switch groups from last week so those students who made the slogan will cut symbols and vice versa. Choose a short slogan such as: God, for the lift of a lifetime; God is the real thing; Natural highs—there's no comparison; God and you, oh what a feeling!

Make your class a place where kids feel safe and comfortable enough to share their feelings and problems. Close today's session by having kids form a circle. Thank God for each of your special, wonderful students and enjoy a group hug.

The Choice Is Mine ✓

Kids make choices to use drugs to satisfy three basic needs. In the spaces below, list some wise choices to meet that need next to the "Thumbs Up", and some unwise choices next to the "Thumbs Down".

✔ I'll See It When I Believe It!

DON (or DAWN) PHILAHUE: Let's give a warm welcome to Gideon!

GIDEON: Thank you Don. It's a pleasure to be here.

DON: First of all, Gideon, let's get a little background. Tell us about yourself.

GIDEON: Our people, the Israelites, considered my family as unimportant nobodies. I was only a farm boy and I felt like the biggest zero of all.

DON: Is it correct to say you had an inferiority complex?

GIDEON: I sure did. But that's not the worst part. Our nation was in great trouble. Enemies destroyed all our crops and stole our animals. We had to hide in caves and were starving to death.

DON: How did you turn all that around to become a great leader and save your people?

GIDEON: It all started one day when I was standing in a pit in the ground and. . .

DON: Wait a minute. What were you doing in a pit?

GIDEON: Hiding. I was feeling low, slow, weak, depressed and scared to death. Then all of a sudden an angel told me the Lord was with me. He even called me a mighty warrior. My knees were shaking so badly that I could hardly stand up.

DON: I'll bet you were surprised.

GIDEON: You can say that again! I couldn't see how God could be with me when I was having so much trouble. But then I realized that it was really God speaking to me.

DON: What did He say?

GIDEON: He told me that I was to save the people from their enemies. God said that He was sending me and would be with me.

DON: So you courageously gathered a large army and went to battle?

GIDEON: Not exactly. I did get a lot of men together, but they were as scared as I was. They didn't really trust me and couldn't agree on anything. So God told me to send home everybody who was afraid.

DON: Did many leave?

GIDEON: I'll say! Over twenty thousand of my army turned tail and ran home. I was left with only three-hundred soldiers but God said that was all I needed. He would do the rest.

DON: You must have been very brave to lead such a small army to battle.

GIDEON: I was terrified! The enemy army was humongous! The night we were to attack, my friend and I sneaked up to the enemy camp to spy on them.

DON: What did you find out?

GIDEON: We overheard a soldier talking about a dream he had. His friend said it meant that I was going to defeat them. I thanked God for His assurance right there. We raced back to camp and roused our troops for war.

DON: How did the battle go?

GIDEON: We surrounded the enemy, blew our trumpets and shouted, "For the Lord and for Gideon!" Then we smashed clay jars and held up burning torches. The Lord caused the enemy to get so confused and scared they either killed each other or ran away. We ended up soundly defeating them.

DON: What advice would you give young people who are facing hard problems?

GIDEON: Turn to God to help you. He CAN and WILL do great things for you. You'll see it when you believe it!

Activity Sheet by Bev Gundersen © 1991 David C. Cook Publishing Co. Permission granted to reproduce for classroom use only.

Lesson 3

Read My Lips-No Drugs

Aim: That your students will use God's power to help them refuse harmful substances.
Scripture: Daniel 1:1-20
Unit Verse: My God will meet all your needs according to his glorious riches in Christ Jesus. Philippians 4:19
Unit Affirmation: I CAN SAY NO TO DRUGS!

 Planning Ahead

1. Photocopy activity sheets (pages 31 and 32)-one for each student.
2. Prepare a set of cards for the matching game in SETTING THE STAGE by cutting 3" x 5" cards in half and writing the following words on them, making two cards of each word: Marijuana, Stimulants, Amphetamines, Cocaine, Caffeine, Depressants, Barbiturates, Tranquilizers, Inhalants, Narcotics, Codeine, Morphine, Heroin, Methadone. Make one set of cards for every two or four students.
3. Sew last week's block to Unit Verse add-on banner.

1 Setting the Stage (5-10 minutes)
WHAT YOU'LL DO
- Play a match game to review the key words for this unit
WHAT YOU'LL NEED
- Match game cards

2 Introducing the Issue (20 minutes)
WHAT YOU'LL DO
- Use an activity sheet and read a fable to illustrate the ways kids are most typically offered drugs
- Prepare a fable as a presentation for another class
- Add a phrase to the Unit Affirmation poster
WHAT YOU'LL NEED
- "The Trap" Activity Sheet (page 31)
- Yarn, paper punch, a set of animal puppets (optional)
- Unit Affirmation poster

3 Searching the Scriptures (20 minutes)
WHAT YOU'LL DO
- Participate in a mad-lib story to discover what happens when God helps someone say "No!"
- Use role-plays to rehearse ways to refuse drugs
WHAT YOU'LL NEED
- Bibles
- "The Choices Of A New Generation," Activity Sheet (page 32)

4 Living the Lesson (5-10 minutes)
WHAT YOU'LL DO
- Make a block for the add-on banner
WHAT YOU'LL NEED
- 12" burlap square, felt, markers, scissors, white craft glue

✔ Setting the Stage (5-10 minutes)

As your students arrive today, give a set of the matching cards to every two to four kids. Instruct them to play by shuffling the cards and placing them face down on the table. Each player takes a turn by turning over two cards and reading the words printed on them. If they match, he or she can remove the cards and keep them, and then take another turn. If they do not match, turn them face down again, and the next player takes a turn. Continue until all the matches have been made. The player with the most cards is the winner.

Let's look at the words on the cards for a few moments. We studied about them in the first lesson. What can you tell me about them? Guide your students to briefly review the meaning of each term (see Lesson 1 for information). One way you could do this is by taking out the category words (Stimulants, Depressants, Inhalants, and Narcotics) and laying them on the table. Then place the remainder of the terms in the proper category. As they do this, they might recall other terms that were not included in the game, as well. **These are important words for us to remember if we are going to be "Drug Wise!"**

✔ Introducing the Issue (20 minutes)

Even though there are so many people telling kids about the dangers of using drugs, it's obvious that many thousands use them anyway. How does this happen? How do kids get connected with drugs in the first place? Let kids respond. **Have you or anyone you know ever been offered drugs?** Give opportunity for those in your group who may want to share personal experiences.

Distribute copies of the activity sheet "The Trap" (page 31). Let kids follow along as you read this fable to them. Use a lot of expression to capture their imaginations. **What was the danger that faced the little beaver?** (The trappers upstream.) **Do you think they could have swum upstream and *not* gotten caught in a trap?** (Sure.) **So why would the beavers' parents have told them to stay out of the Upstream waters altogether?** (Didn't want them to take the chance of being caught at all. They thought it was better just to stay completely away.) **Do you think the parents gave good advice, or over-reacted?** Allow for responses. **What does this fable tell us about how kids get "trapped" into using drugs?** Make the point that kids can be drawn into drug use in several ways. They can be approached by strangers (the otter). However, most kids are drawn into using drugs by friends who they know and

trust. **What reasons did the Beaver give himself for choosing to go Up-stream?** (He didn't want to be left alone, he trusted his friend's judgement, thought it would be safe since his friend had been there and said it was.)
What might happen if the little beaver continues to swim upstream? (He might get caught right away because he doesn't know how to identify the traps; he might be OK for awhile, and then get careless about looking for them.)

Every fable has a moral (point it is trying to make). What do you think is the moral of this story? Allow kids to make suggestions. One possibility: Friends can be more dangerous than strangers! Have them write a moral on the bottom of the activity sheet.

Since it is kids who most often lead other kids into using drugs, it is kids who can best tell other kids *not* to use drugs. For the next few minutes, involve your class in preparing a presentation to share with another class about the dangers of using drugs. Depending on the size of your class, choose one or more of the following projects:

1. Prepare the fable, "The Trap" as a play or a puppet show. If possible, have available a set of animal puppets for this project and have the kids make a simple backdrop for the show. Another possibility is for them to act the parts, making simple animal props to wear or carry.

2. The artists in your class may like to put "The Trap" into a story book. They can divide the fable into 4 or 5 scenes and have a different person take each one and make a page for the book. Then use the hole punch and yarn to assemble the pages.

3. Your more creative writers could write another fable, portraying a differ-ent aspect of the drug abuse problem. For example, they could write a story about a rabbit who becomes so obsessed with eating carrots that he no longer wants anything to do with his friends. This new fable could also be produced as a puppet show, play or story book.

4. The musical souls in your midst might want to write a song that would communicate a message against drug use. They can use an existing song and write new words, or create both the words and music.

When the projects are completed, gather your class together again and ask each group to share their creation with the rest of the class. Be sure to give lots of affirmation for their efforts.

OPTIONAL: If possible, make arrangements for your kids to actually visit another class to share their work. Telling the class about this before they get started will add significantly to their motivation to do a good job.

Display the Unit Affirmation Poster and read the Affirmation together aloud. Ask the class to think of a new phrase for the third line. A possibility is, ". . . even if it means saying NO to a friend." **It can be hard to stand up for what we believe to be right. It's always easier to give in and go with the group than to take a strong stand. The Bible tells us about someone who had the same problem. Let's see what happened when he said NO!**

✓ Searching the Scriptures (20 minutes)

Start today's Bible study by announcing that you are going to read a "mad-lib" story. These are stories with blank spaces where words have been omitted. In this story the words in the parenthesis will tell you what kind of words to put in the blanks.

For the first blank, have someone give you a boy's name. Write that student's suggestion in the blank. Ask someone else to name a foreign country. Continue going around the class with students giving suggestions until all the blanks are filled. Don't give away the context of the story. Remind your kids that a verb is an action word—run, choose. An adjective describes something or somebody—smart, tall. When all the blanks are filled, read the story aloud.

Once upon a time a boy named (boy's name) was kidnapped and taken to live in (foreign country). He and his three friends , (names of three boys) were taken to live in a (dwelling place). They were taught (school subject) and (school subject). Every day they were given (food) and (beverage) by their captors. Now the (number) boys had decided not to eat or drink these things because they were not good for their bodies. So they (verb in past tense) to the (government official) and said, "Please don't make us take these things." But the man was (emotion) and wouldn't agree. "Let us try an experiment for (number) days," the boys begged. "Just give us (food) to eat and (beverage) to drink. Then (one of our five senses) how we do. The man (verb in past tense), "OK, but this had better work!" At the end of the time, these boys were more (adjective) than all the others. " (exclamation)," the people said. "These guys are really (adjective)!"

Have you ever heard a Bible story like that one? Today we're going to talk about someone who stood up to a king and refused to be pressured into doing something he knew was wrong. Although we probably won't ever have to face an influential government leader like he did, this lesson will show us how to overcome a powerful temptation that all of face today. Let's turn to Daniel 1:1-20 and see what really happened. Have students take turns reading the story.

What were some of the things the king did to try to make Daniel and

his friends more like the Babylonians? (Make them learn his language, changed their names, change their eating habits.) Explain that the Babylonian education included learning magic and alchemy. Alchemy was an early form of chemistry whose chief objectives were to change common metals into gold, discover the secret of perpetual youth and how to change the forms of humans. All these things are sorcery and were forbidden by God.

All of the boy's Jewish names contained the name of God. For example, Daniel means "God is my judge." Their new names had a connection with heathen idols. Daniel's name, Belteshazzar, never stuck. We know him best as Daniel.

Why do you think Daniel was so outspoken against eating the king's food? God's laws about food were very specific. The food they were now given had been offered to idols. To partake of it was to surrender to a pagan society and compromise all your dedication to God. What appeared harmless on the surface was a test of conformity to the world.

How did these Hebrew young men compare with the others at the end of the training period? (There was no one equal to them; they were ten times better than all the heathen sorcerers.) Emphasize that God honors those who honor Him.

Divide your class into four teams. Distribute copies of the activity sheet "The Choices Of A New Generation" (page 32). Assign one of the situations to each team and let them take a few minutes to work out a role-play for it. Team members who don't act out the roles can brainstorm other ways these same situations might be handled. Have them write these down and be prepared to share them with the class. If you have a small class, students could do more than one role-play. You may want to have students switch roles to provide more insight into the problem. Involve all the students in the role-play by telling them they must be good observers who will be expected to share their insights in the follow-up discussions.

Discuss each role-play. **What do you think each character was feeling? Why do you think they acted the way they did? What makes us act or think like that? What are some other ways this problem could be handled?** Students who brainstormed this last question can share their lists now.

Talk about ways to handle peer pressure situations. Some tips are: Identify any potential troubles that might arise from acceptance. Think through the consequences of your decision. Take quick and effective action. Choose a response such as suggesting doing something else or changing the subject entirely. State your answer positively and strongly to show that you mean it. You must get out of the situation within thirty seconds or you will be influ-

enced to go along with the trouble.

Because you have to act quickly to avoid being trapped in a potentially harmful situation, you need to be like Daniel. He had decided to be faithful to the Lord before he was faced with the problem of eating food that had been offered to idols. It is much easier to resist temptations if you have already decided where to draw the line and say "No!"

Have students turn to Philippians 4:19 and read it together. **When you are in a situation where you are faced with a temptation to take drugs, you can ask God to give you the strength and wisdom to resist pressure and do the right thing. Because He has promised to supply all your needs, you can trust Him to help you reject Satan's temptations.**

Living the Lesson (5-10 minutes)

Work on today's block for the add-on banner. Pass out the materials. Select a brief caption such as, Refuse to abuse; or Nope to dope. Let half of the class cut out felt letters or plan to write it on the burlap. The other students will decide what symbols to use for the slogan and cut the felt pieces for it. Glue all pieces on the block.

Today you learned some good ways to say "no" to drugs. We talked about the need to decide to refuse to take drugs before you are tempted. I'm going to give you a few minutes to do that now. Close your eyes and pray silently. Allow a brief time for this. Those of you who decided *not* to take drugs can show that by giving your pledge to the Lord. Place your right hand over your heart and pray this pledge after me. **Say this prayer-pledge aloud, pausing to allow your students to repeat it. "Dear Lord, because my body is Your temple, I promise not to dishonor it by taking harmful drugs. Thank You for providing for all my needs. In Jesus' name I pray. Amen."**

The Trap

Once upon a time, there was a young beaver who loved to swim in the river outside his dam. Every morning he would play water games with his friends in the pool near his home. Soon the young beavers began to venture further away, enjoying the excitement of exploring new waters.

One day, the beaver's parents sat him down to have a serious talk. "Now that you're old enough to swim in waters beyond our pool, it's time we tell you about the dangers that lie in the world of the Upstream River Country.

"Dangers?" the young beaver didn't understand.

"Oh, yes," his parents continued. "In the river country not so far from here live humans who set traps for unsuspecting beavers. When they catch us, they send us off to make coats out of our fur! Stay in the downstream country. We couldn't stand to lose you to the trappers!"

The young beaver took his parents' words seriously and even told his friends about them. Their parents had told them the same thing, and for many weeks they played happily in the downstream waters. Until one day when a playful otter joined them.

"Hi!" he called out. "Boy, are you missing all the fun! The waters UPSTREAM are ever so much more fun to play in! Hey, I'm going back there right now! Why don't you join me?"

The little beavers looked horrified. "No way, man! Don't you know about the trappers up there?"

"Sure, but they won't hurt you! Just stay away from the traps! Only dumb animals get caught in the traps. Come on!"

The beavers looked at each other. Were the Upstream waters safe after all? "No way," he replied. And he and his friends swam away. They knew that trusting parents was much smarter than trusting strangers.

Many weeks later, the little beaver went out to play one morning, as usual. He met his friends and they began to swim downstream.

"Just a minute," one of his buddies called out. "Let's go Upstream and play today."

The little beaver looked confused. "Hey, I thought we had that settled! No playing Upstream."

"I know there are traps there," the friend replied. "But I've been there and look at me! I'm OK, aren't I? And I gotta tell you! The otter was right! It's REALLY fun up there! Come on, let's go!"

Now the beaver was really confused. All his friends were turning to swim upstream. He felt scared, but he didn't want to be left alone. "Well," he thought to himself, "this isn't a stranger. This is my good friend. And if he's been there and come back, it must be all right. I'll just try it out!" He turned around in the water. "Hey, wait for me!" he shouted after them.

THE MORAL OF THE STORY IS _____

The Choices of a New Generation

1. You are at a party. The host hands you a can of beer. What will you say?

_____

_____

_____

_____

2. One of the most popular kids in school offers you a joint (marijuana). What will you do?

_____

_____

_____

_____

3. You have been studying late and are tired. A friend offers you some amphetamines (uppers) to pep you up. What will you say?_____

_____

_____

_____

4. You are at a friend's house. He offers you a bottle of typewriter correction fluid and tells you inhaling its fumes will make you feel great. What will you do?

_____

_____

_____

_____

Lesson 4

Family Matters

Aim: That your students will seek God's comfort and power in families where there is substance abuse.
Scripture: II Timothy 2:22-26
Unit Verse: My God will meet all your needs according to his glorious riches in Christ Jesus. Philippians 4:19
Unit Affirmation: I CAN SAY NO TO DRUGS!

 Planning Ahead

1. Photocopy activity sheets (pages 39 and 40)–one for each student.
2. Collect "junk" for the sculptures in SETTING THE STAGE. Items can include empty candy wrappers, used pencils, paper cups, paper clips, twigs and leaves, pebbles/rocks, and any other little things you find available in your house or yard.
3. Make a comparison chart as described in SEARCHING THE SCRIPTURES.
4. Attach by sewing or gluing last week's block to Unit Verse add-on banner.

 1 Setting the Stage (5-10 minutes)

WHAT YOU'LL DO

- Make Junk Sculptures as a way to illustrate family balance and stability.

WHAT YOU'LL NEED

- A bag of "junk"

2 Introducing the Issue (20 minutes)

WHAT YOU'LL DO

- Use an activity sheet to discuss the effects of family chemical dependency on children
- Participate in a Family Sculpture activity to portray families affected by chemical dependency
- Add a phrase to the Unit Affirmation poster

WHAT YOU'LL NEED

- "It's My Problem, Too!" Activity Sheet (page 39)
- Unit Affirmation poster

 3 Searching the Scriptures (20 minutes)

WHAT YOU'LL DO

- Understand how God can help me deal with any problems caused by substance abuse in my family by developing tips drawn from biblical principles

WHAT YOU'LL NEED

- Bibles

 4 Living the Lesson (5-10 minutes)

WHAT YOU'LL DO

- Use an activity sheet to write prescriptions for hurting kids to show how they can use God's help to cope with substance abuse in their family
- Make a block for the add-on banner

WHAT YOU'LL NEED

- "Where Does It Hurt?" Activity Sheet (page 40)
- One 12-inch burlap square, felt, scissors, markers, white craft glue

 *Lesson 4*

SPECIAL NOTE: As you work through this lesson be alert and sensitive to students who may be living with an addictive parent. These kids appear to be insecure, cautious, fearful or mistrusting. Many times they can't express their own true feelings. Their real feelings may be hidden under behavior problems. They are living in a personal world of fear, helplessness, and uncertainty and desperately need God's help and yours.

Be available to listen, encourage and support. Help the child understand the addiction is not his or her fault. Do not condemn the alcoholic parent because this makes the child feel disloyal. If you think it would be beneficial, suggest a peer support group such as Alatots or Alateens. Sharing experiences sometimes helps people find ways to cope better with their problems. Counseling with a reliable counselor is sometimes helpful. In an addictive home, everyone suffers, not only the addict.

✓ Setting the Stage (5-10 minutes)

Before your students arrive today, place the bag of "junk" on the table. Add a few basics, like glue, paper and markers. As the kids come in, instruct them to get right to work on making a sculpture using the supplies on the table. It can be as large or small as they want, but they must use only what is on the table. You might consider adding some incentive by telling them you will be judging them when they are complete. You can give recognition for things such as the biggest, smallest, neatest, messiest, most stable, shakiest, etc. Make it light and fun!

Look at the variety in our sculptures! No two are alike, some are small, some large, some very secure and some look like they will topple over at any moment! In many ways, families are like these sculptures; some are large, some small, some very secure and some shaky. Today we want to talk about drug abuse and families and how using chemicals affect not only the person using them, but the entire family group (sculpture)!

✓ Introducing the Issue (20 minutes)

Families are more than just a collection of people who live together. They are more like our sculptures; all the pieces are connected and influence each other. When something happens to one member, all the

others are affected. Take one of the sculptures and pull a piece out of it. If possible, choose one that will make a dramatic difference in the sculpture, perhaps even make it collapse. **That's how it is when a family member abuses drugs or alcohol. Someone may say, "It's my life and my choice. I'm not hurting anyone else by what I'm doing." But that's *not* true. How does a family member's chemical abuse affect the rest of the family?** Allow for responses.

Distribute copies of the activity sheet, "It's My Problem, Too!" (page 39). This activity sheet illustrates some of the effects a child in a chemically dependent home will experience. Ask a volunteer to read the first illustration. Have kids write FAMILY SECRETS on the first line. **Most kids who live in homes with a chemically dependent family member will be told emphatically that *no one* outside of the family should ever find out about the problem. How does that effect the family members who are not abusing alchohol or other drugs?** (Kids will not be able to have friends over to play; they may feel their family is bad; no one in the family can get help to deal with personal feelings.) **Family secrets are heavy burdens for kids to bear!**

Ask a volunteer to read the second illustration. Have kids write UNMET NEEDS on the line. **When a parent abuses chemicals, he or she is not able to function normally and the rest of family must pick up the load. How does that effect children in the family?** (They will often *not* be cared for properly, and they will be asked to assume the neglected adult responsibilities. Even if the abuser is another child in the family, the parents can be so distracted by the problem that they do not care for the "non-problem" kids adequately.)

Ask a volunteer to read the third illustration. Have kids write BROKEN PROMISES on the line. **Family members who are being controlled by alcohol are often unable to follow through on promises made to other family members. They may not remember making them, or they may be unable to function normally at the time. How does that effect other family members?** (They are no longer able to trust the abuser. For kids, when the hurt is deep enough, this can extend to an inability to trust anyone.)

Ask a volunteer to read the fourth illustration. Have kids write FEAR on the line. **Abusing family members are often physically and emotionally violent. Family members are often terrified of the abuser. Kids in this situation must remember two things: 1) It is the chemicals that make the person this way, it's *not* because he or she hates you. 2) Take care of yourself! Your safety comes first. Leave the house or call someone to help.**

Ask a volunteer to read the fifth illustration. Have kids write FEELINGS ARE

NOT OK on the line. **When chemicals control a house, children are often not allowed to express their feelings in normal, healthy ways.**

Use the idea of a sculpture to illustrate the effects of chemicals in a family by creating a family sculpture. Ask for six volunteers. Give each a role (mother, father, son, daughter, grandparents, etc.). **In a normal family, the members interact and are connected to and supportive of one another. How could we make a human sculpture with our family members to illustrate that?** Let kids make suggestions. One possibility is to have them stand in a circle facing each other and holding hands. **However, in homes with chemical abuse, the abuser gets all the attention and the family members are often unable to support and interact with each other. How could we illustrate that?** Let kids form a sculpture. One possibility is to stand the "abuser" on a chair and have the other family members scattered around, looking sad or scared. **What differences do you see in these two families?** Let kids talk about their observations.

Display the Unit Affirmation poster and read the Affirmation aloud together. **In a few minutes we will talk about what we can do when a member of our family abuses chemicals. One thing we *don't* want to do is cope with it by using chemicals ourselves. If someone in your family abuses, you will be four times more at risk of being an abuser than other kids.** Write, ". . . especially if someone in my family is an abuser!" on the fourth line. **Don't take the chance! Find another way to cope. Now let's see if we can discover some better ways to cope.**

Searching the Scriptures (20 minutes)

When people become addicted to a drug, they are no longer in control of their lives. They may think they can stop taking drugs any time but their minds and bodies have been changed by the drugs so that they actually believe they need the drugs to survive. They keep taking them even though they know they are dangerous and harmful. In reality they have been tricked by Satan and become his slaves. As awful and frightening as this is, there is hope. God's Word gives us some ways to take care of ourselves help them. Ask students to turn to II Timothy 2:22-26 in their Bibles. Have students take turns reading these verses.

Display a comparison chart on the board or a large sheet of paper. The chart should have two columns under the titles of "Principle" and "Practice." As you the study the passage together, list each Bible rule in the "principle" column.

What rules do you find in verse 22? (Avoid evil; live right; work for faith, love, and peace with people who trust in the Lord.) **What are you to stay away**

from? (Foolish and stupid arguments.) **Why?** (Because they lead to quarrels.) **What usually happens when people start to argue?** (People start to shout, don't listen, small arguments grow into bigger arguments.) **How does the Bible encourage followers of Jesus to react when people start to argue with them?** (Refuse to quarrel, be kind and patient, teach them gently.) **Why?** (If you are courteous and kind and don't lose your temper, people are more likely to quiet down and listen to you—Proverbs 15:1*.)

II Timothy 2:25, 26 gives some hints of how you can pray for people who are enslaved to sin. What are they? (God can help them repent—change their minds; they can recognize the truth—about themselves as slaves of Satan and about God who loves them and can free them; they can come to their senses; escape from the devil's trap.)

Work with your Juniors to form some suggestions for kids to use with family members who are abusing alcohol or other drugs. List these under the "Practice" section of your comparison chart. As you draw tips from these principles, talk about possible reasons for following them. Some tips are:

1. Don't become addicted yourself. In homes where there is chemical dependency, drugs are often easily obtainable. Juniors who feel helpless to influence or change their situations can feel so despondent they give up and decide, "If you can't lick them, join them." In addition there is some medical evidence that addiction such as alcoholism is a combination of genetics and environment. Children of alcoholics are four times as likely to become alcoholics as those of non-alcoholic parents.

2. Take care of yourself. You are a valuable person and you matter to God. You deserve to be loved, cared for, supported and respected. If your addicted parents are not able to meet these needs, look for helpful places where these needs can be met. You deserve the best!

3. Turn to God and His followers for help. Trusted Christian adults such as teachers, pastors, youth workers, or counselors can be of special help. The church family as a whole can be a support group that provides a loving home for needy kids. Make your classroom a warm, safe place where students can feel acceptance and caring.

4. Ask God to help you respond positively to the person who is addicted. Don't argue and get involved in quarrels, be kind, patient, gentle (sensitive), and not be resentful (bitter).

5. Find constructive ways to express your feelings of anger, sadness, fear. Kids in homes where there is chemical dependency have many feelings of anger, sadness, fear, confusion, helplessness, etc. These can be expressed through talking with a trusted adult, writing down what you're feeling, exercising and blowing off steam, or talking aloud to God. Don't stuff your feelings, get them out.

6. Use the armor of God and spiritual weapons to stand firm. All sin is part of the spiritual battle. Addicts are slaves to sin. Because they are slaves of the devil, who is the leader of spiritual darkness, be sure to use the armor of God (Ephesians 6:11*) and spiritual weapons. (II Corinthians 10:3-5.*) Review these weapons: truth; having a right relationship with God ourselves; peace; hope; faith; prayer; God's Word; sharing the good news of the help and freedom God can give them through His Son, Jesus.

7. Consider doing an intervention. Truth can be a powerful weapon. This is seen in intervention. Under the guidance of people trained to work with people with addictions, people close to the addict openly confront him or her as a group with evidences of the addiction. They then express their genuine love and concern for that individual and urge him or her to seek help.

OPTIONAL: If you have a longer class period, have students look up starred verses and read them aloud at the appropriate places in the discussion.

Distribute copies of the activity sheet "Where Does It Hurt?" (page 40) and ask someone to read the instructions. Divide the class into three teams. Have each team work on one problem using the tips they formulated from the biblical principles. Allow a few minutes for this, circulating from group to group so you can give necessary help. Have teams share their suggestions with the group. Be sure to emphasize things such as: kids are not responsible for a parent's addiction; seeking adult help; the value of talking about problems with those who understand and care; the need to stop repressing true feelings and identifying and expressing true ones.

✔ Living the Lesson (5-10 minutes)

Display the add-on banner. Have students repeat the Unit Verse together. **God understands all about the problems that homes with chemical dependency have. He knows that when one member is addicted, all the family suffers. You can tell Him all your hurts and use His Word to help you. He loves you and wants to be your forever, Heavenly Father. He promises to supply all your needs and He always keeps His promises.**

Distribute materials and work on the block for the banner. Decide on a slogan such as: Hugs, not drugs; I can talk about what hurts. Half of the class will do the slogan while the other half makes the illustration for it. Glue both slogan and symbols to the burlap block.

Close by singing some familiar song such as "I'm So Glad I'm A Part of the Family Of God" or "Blest Be The Tie That Binds."

It's My Problem, Too! ✔

1. _____

"Don't you tell ANYONE about your brother being arrested for drunk driving!"

2. _____

"Be a dear and fix supper for everyone again. Mommy still doesn't feel good."

3. _____

"This is the third week in a row you promised you'd take me to the ball game."
"Sorry, sport. We'll do it next week. Promise."

4. _____

"I ought to give you one good whipping; that's what you need!"

5. _____

"I'm afraid!"
"That's silly; there's nothing to be afraid of!"

Where Does It Hurt?

Each of the situations on this page expresses the feelings of kids who live in homes where there is some form of chemical dependency. Read each problem and write out a prescription for it in the space given.

My mom seems like two different people. When she's not taking drugs, she's nice to us and we have good times together. But when she's been taking drugs, she acts real weird. It's like she forgets all about us kids. I have to do most of the work and take care of my little brother and baby sister. I have trouble getting my homework done because I have so much to do at home. My teacher says if my grades don't improve, she'll have to flunk me. I wonder if it's all my fault. If I was a better student, maybe Mom wouldn't use drugs.

_____

_____

My dad drinks a lot. When he does that, he yells and fights and sometimes even hits us. I tried to hide his bottle once, but he found it anyway. He said if I ever tried that again, he would make me wish I hadn't. I'm scared all the time. When he's drunk I'm scared that he will really hurt one of us. When he's not drinking, I'm scared wondering what he will do the next time.

_____

_____

I really enjoy the kids club at church. Last week the teacher brought me home after the meeting. She said she would like to meet my parents. I was worried that Dad might be drinking, but I felt like I had to tell her to come in. I hoped everything would be OK. I introduced her to my mom. Then Dad came out of the kitchen. He had been drinking a lot. He made a crude remark about my teacher. Then he offered her a can of beer. She was real polite and left in a hurry. I feel terrible about it. I sometimes pretend that Dad is like other fathers and there's nothing wrong. But now I guess everybody will know he's not.

_____

_____

How Can I Help You?

Aim: That your students will have the desire to reach out in God's love to help their friends who abuse substances

Scripture: Titus 2:11-3:8

Unit Verse: My God will meet all your needs according to his glorious riches in Christ Jesus. Philippians 4:19

Unit Affirmation: I CAN SAY NO TO DRUGS!

 Planning Ahead

1. Photocopy activity sheets, (pages 47 and 48)–one for each student.
2. Gather about 20 simple objects for the memory game in SETTING THE STAGE. These can be anything you have around the house: a rubber band, a book, a spoon, a letter opener, etc. Vary the sizes from very small to large, and include some common and some unique objects. A one-minute timer would also be useful.
3. Attach by sewing or gluing last week's block to Unit Verse add-on banner.
4. Prepare Factionary Game with six 3"x 5" cards as described in SEARCHING THE SCRIPTURES.

1 Setting the Stage (5-10 minutes)

WHAT YOU'LL DO

- Play a memory game to illustrate the need to be observant concerning friends who may abuse chemicals

WHAT YOU'LL NEED

- 20 objects
- Optional: a one-minute timer

2 Introducing the Issue (20 minutes)

WHAT YOU'LL DO

- Use an activity sheet to identify the signs of chemical abuse
- See an illustration of how signs of abuse form patterns we can identify
- Complete the Unit Affirmation poster

WHAT YOU'LL NEED

- "Watch Out!" Activity Sheet (page 47)
- Jigsaw puzzle pieces, picture of the complete jigsaw puzzle
- Unit Affirmation poster

3 Searching the Scriptures (20 minutes)

WHAT YOU'LL DO

- Play "Factionary" to learn theological terms used in the Scripture passage
- Use an activity sheet to discover Bible principles for helping friends who are trapped in substance abuse
- Optional: See an object lesson that pictures how the completed work of salvation is transferred to undeserving people

WHAT YOU'LL NEED

- Bibles
- "Factionary" game cards
- "God Squad Alert" Activity Sheet (page 48)
- Optional: 12" piece of string

4 Living the Lesson (5-10 minutes)

WHAT YOU'LL DO

- Brainstorm ways to help friends who abuse drugs
- Make a block for the add-on banner

WHAT YOU'LL NEED

- One 12" burlap square, felt, scissors, white craft glue, markers

41

Setting the Stage (5-10 minutes)

Before your students arrive, place the objects for the memory game in the middle of your table or in an open space on the floor. As kids enter the room, direct their attention to the objects and tell them to carefully observe all of them and where they are located. They are not to touch them or move them. When everyone has arrived, divide the group into two teams. To play, the members of the first team turns their backs, covers their eyes, or leaves the room while the second team takes away several objects and hides them. Then use the timer to give the first team one minute to figure out which objects are missing. When time runs out, give them ten points if they identified all the objects correctly. Repeat the process for the second team. You can play as many rounds as time allows, adding variety by mixing up the placement of the objects and the number of objects removed each time.

What skills were necessary to play this game well? (Memory and observation skills are the most important.) **Today we are going to talk about helping our friends who may get trapped in chemical abuse. As we'll see, the first thing we need is to have good memory and observation skills so we will notice when friends show signs of abuse!**

Introducing the Issue (20 minutes)

Even though many people are working very hard to keep kids from abusing chemicals, far too many kids will make unwise choices and get trapped by drug and alcohol abuse every year. All of you will know someone who will get into trouble this way. People who become trapped in abuse cannot get out by themselves. They need our help. What can we do if we suspect something is going on with a friend? Let kids share initial reactions. The first step is to learn how to recognize chemical abuse in others so we will be aware that a friend is in need of help.

Distribute copies of the activity sheet "Watch Out!" (page 47). This sheet shows the path kids take to becoming addicted to chemicals, and some of the sign posts that point the way. By being familiar with the signs, we can tell when friends may be in a dangerous place. As a class, fill in the blanks using the following information.

Sign post #1: ASKS QUESTIONS. Showing an unusual amount of curiosity about drugs may be a beginning warning sign.

Sign post #2: TALKS ABOUT USE. Curiosity turns to talking about others who are using. May know of many situations where kids are getting and using drugs.

Sign post #3: REPORTS USE. Hearing a friend talk about trying drugs for themselves is a clear danger sign.

"JUST TESTING" HOUSE: LIMITATIONS - ONE TIME ONLY; CURIOSITY SATIS-FIED. For one reason or another, many kids will try drugs one or two times. At that point, their curiosity is satisfied and they have no interest in using again.

Sign post #4: NEW FRIENDS. A continued interest in drugs may mean a new group of friends who are "into" using chemicals.

Sign post #5: CHANGES IN MOODS AND APPEARANCE. The changes may be noticeable, but so subtle friends wonder what's going on but never suspect drug use.

Sign post #6: USES REGULARLY. May not be everyday, but alcohol or other drugs become an on-going part of life.

"PARTY TIME" HOUSE: LIMITATIONS - USES ONLY AT PARTIES AND WITH FRIENDS. Kids at this stage use as a response to peer pressure and to belong to the group.

Sign post #7: DRAMATIC CHANGES. When abuse goes beyond social use, dramatic changes in appearance and behavior will emerge. Missing school, dropping grades, quitting favorite activities, hangovers and other physical signs of being high are some of the changes to look for.

Sign post #8: LOSS OF INTEREST IN FRIENDS. As chemicals take over, the person becomes more and more interested in being alone and begins avoiding non-abusing friends.

Sign post #9: CARRIES DRUGS. As the addiction grows, kids will keep their drugs or alcohol with them. Friends may discover them carrying or even using chemicals.

"ADDICTION" HOUSE: CHARACTERISTICS - PHYSICAL AND EMOTIONAL DEPENDENCE. When addiction occurs, the person feels physical and/or emotional pain when he or she is not high.

Sign post #10: LIE, CHEAT, STEAL. As the addiction grows, kids will do anything to get their supply of chemicals!

Sign post #11: CAN'T FUNCTION. In the deepest levels of addiction, kids *have to have* drugs to function at all. They cannot face life without them.

Although watching for signs of drug abuse in friends is important, we must realize that just showing a few of the signs we just talked about does *not* necessarily mean a friend is hooked on drugs. For instance, everyone is a little curious about drugs and we all experience changes in moods and appearance from time to time. What we are looking for is patterns of behavior that show many of the signs over a period of time. Take out several pieces of the jigsaw puzzle you brought, but do *not* let the kids see the picture on the box. **Here are a few pieces of a puzzle. Who can tell me what the puzzle picture is, just by looking at these pieces?** Let kids guess, if they like. Then show the box lid. **Were you even close? You couldn't possibly know what the big picture was until you put many of the pieces together. It's the same with**

watching for the signs of drug abuse. A few signs don't mean we need to accuse a friend of abuse. But if you observe a pattern developing or know the friend is using, you can make a move to do something!

Display the Unit Affirmation poster and say the Affirmation aloud together. Since this is the last week, review the information on the first four lines. Add to the last line, ". . . and help my friends say NO, too!" **Now let's look to God's Word to discover some things we can do to help our friends who are *not* saying NO to alcohol and other drugs.**

 Searching the Scriptures (20 minutes)

Today's Scripture passage contains some terms Juniors may not understand. Play a game of "Factionary" to introduce them to these words. Before class, write one term at the top of each card. Below it give definitions. A suggested list is: GRACE— 1) God's kindness and love given to undeserving people 2) God's kindness earned by doing good deeds; UPRIGHT—1) overly strict; 2) honorable, trustworthy; REDEEM—1) trade off, turn in; 2) rescue, free, deliver; MALICE—1) desire or deliberate action to harm another 2) bondage, slavery; SAVE—1) put away money, economize 2) rescue from harm or danger; JUSTIFIED—1) accused, judged 2) made right with God. Distribute these cards and have students mark the definition they think is correct. Discuss these terms together.

When you discover your friends are abusing substances, you want to help them. But what can you do? People who abuse drugs are no longer in control of their lives. They have been tricked by the devil into becoming his slaves. But God's Word gives us some ways we can help those who are under his control. Have students turn to Titus 2:11-3:8 in their Bibles and take turns reading these verses. The activity sheet (page 48) will help put the biblical principles in this passage into perspective in regards to the problem of how to help friends who are abusing drugs.

Distribute copies of the activity sheet "God Squad Alert" (page 48). This skit is about a team of Christian kids who fight evil. You will need four people to take the parts. Today we're going to meet a team of young people who are dedicated to fighting evil wherever they find it. As today's scene opens, we find them gathered in team headquarters, discussing the latest alert—a friend whom they suspect is using drugs.

Read through the skit. Those who don't have a part can follow along on their activity sheets. Discuss the play together, comparing it with the Scripture passage. List the biblical principles on the board or a large sheet of paper as you go along. **Who can accept God's grace and salvation?** (Everyone; even druggies.)

According to these Bible verses, what are followers of Jesus to say "NO"

to? (Ungodliness and worldly passions; evil things the world wants to do.) **What do you think some of these evil things are?** (Using alcohol and other drugs, stealing, lying, speaking evil of others, hurting people.) **Instead, how are Christians to live?** (Doing good things to help others; teaching, encouraging, and reminding people to be obedient to authorities; living in peace; being gentle and understanding with others.)

What can we tell people about salvation that will be an encouragement to them when they are fighting with addiction? (Jesus Christ is the Savior; God makes us right with Himself by grace—not by earning it through doing good deeds, but to undeserving people who trust in Jesus; God loves them and they don't have to have their "act together" to come to Jesus.)

OPTIONAL: If you have a longer class time, use this object lesson to demonstrate what Jesus did for us when He died on the cross. You will need a piece of string about twelve inches long. Lay the string on the table in front of you. Fold your

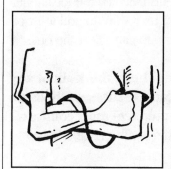  arms across your chest. Keep your arms folded, grasp the left end of the string with your right hand and the right end with your left hand. Hold on to the ends of the string and unfold your arms. The string is knotted without letting go of the ends! Jesus has done all the work of salvation for you. When you ask Him to be your Savior, God's forgiveness is transferred to you.

Who has the power to help us overcome Satan and the hold he has on people through addiction? (The Holy Spirit.) **How do we get the Holy Spirit?** (By asking God to forgive our sins and trusting in Jesus as our Savior.) Titus 3:5 speaks of rebirth and renewal. To help students see how this works in the lives of people who abuse drugs, have someone look up II Corinthians 5:17 and read it aloud. **What difference would this make for someone enslaved by drugs?** (The Holy Spirit empowers people to lay aside their old way of life and begin again. It may not happen instantly, but with God's help they can be free from their addiction.)

Point out that just saying no to drugs won't take care of people's emotional needs. Only Jesus can bring real happiness; self-worth, a sense of belonging; understanding and love. Have someone look up John 10:10 and read it aloud. **What kind of life does Jesus want us to have?** (Full, overflowing, more satisfying

than before.)

What's your opinion about telling someone if you suspect your friend is using drugs? Assist students to understand that sometimes telling a trusted adult about friends who are using drugs is the best way to help. **You wouldn't hesitate to tell someone if your friend was going to be run down by a train, would you? Abusing substances is far more dangerous than being run over. Your friend may be angry and break off the friendship, but if she or he is in trouble it is the most loving thing you can do. You may be saving his or her life.**

✓ Living the Lesson (5-10 minutes)

Ask students to brainstorm ways they can help friends who use drugs. Encourage them to come up with as many different ways as possible. Emphasize that at this point you want quantity, not quality. Don't let students evaluate the ideas until they run dry of suggestions. In addition to the "do's" you may want to add a list of "don'ts." After all the ideas are listed on the board, the group can select the ones that would work best.

Distribute paper and pencils. **As you look at the list(s) here, think about any friends you feel may be using drugs and how you can use these methods to help them. Make a personal list of ways that you would feel most comfortable using.** Allow a few minutes for this before proceeding with the Unit Verse activity.

Display the add-on banner. Have students say the verse together. **When you honestly want to help your friend stop using drugs, God will help you. He can help you accept your friend without condemning him/her for using drugs. He can give you guidance as to what to say and love to say it in a gentle, caring way. If you think you need to tell someone, He can help you do that also. Most of all, by sharing your best friend, Jesus, you can let your friend know there is hope for a better, more fully satisfying life.**

Distribute the materials for today's block. Choose a slogan such as Say "No!" to drugs, Say "Yes!" to Jesus. The kids who worked on the symbol last week can make the slogan today and vice versa. Glue the pieces on the burlap square. Even though today is the last lesson on substance abuse, add this block to the banner and display it in your classroom next week.

Have students pray silently for friends they are concerned about. **Remember Jesus loves them so much He gave His life to bring them a full and satisfying life free from the evil slavery of drugs.** Close by praying aloud, asking God's help for your students as they reach out in love to their needy friends.

Watch Out!

Watching for the signs of chemical abuse in our friends and knowing what to do when we see them, is part of being a caring friend.

✔ God Squad Alert

(Team Members: IQ; Tiger; Vibes; and Amen.)

VIBES: I feel that Jon is not only taking drugs, but really abusing them. We just have to do something to help him!

TIGER: How about if I grab him after school, twist his arm, shake him up and tell him to shape up or else?

IQ: I could patch into the school computer and put a note on his file that said "Druggie." That would alert the principal who'd notify his parents and he would get the help he needs.

AMEN: Hold on. There are a lot of things we can do. But what *should* we do? How would Jesus want us to handle this problem? He cares even more about Jon than we do.

TIGER: You mean check it out in God's Word and find some tips?

AMEN: Right! Remember last week when we were studying Titus 2:11-3:8? Well, I think that might give us some guidelines.

VIBES: I've got it here. It says that God's grace, the grace that can save, is for everyone. That means God loves druggies too.

TIGER: Paul says in verse 12 that we shouldn't do the evil things of the world. Instead we are to be self-controlled and to live God's way. I guess Jesus wouldn't strong-arm Jon, would He?

AMEN: I doubt it. Jesus gave His life to free us from all evil. That means He can break the power of drugs in Jon's life.

VIBES: That would make Jon feel good,

wouldn't it? He would know that God will help him do the right things.

AMEN: Do you see that in verse 15 we are to encourage people like Jon?

IQ: When Paul says we are to rebuke them, I think that must mean correct them with love; because we really care for them and want the best for them.

TIGER: We can remind them that using drugs is against the law.

AMEN: Hmm, Paul says that we shouldn't slander anyone. What do you think that means, IQ?

IQ: Slander means saying or writing bad things that ruin someone's reputation or character. I guess that includes computer notes on school files. Paul also says we should be peaceable. Guess I wasn't very smart after all.

VIBES: These verses tell us to be considerate. I know if I were in Jon's place I'd want someone to be kind and gentle to me.

AMEN: We think that some sins are a lot worse than others and that God hesitates to forgive them. But the truth is that we are all sinners. Jesus saves us because of His mercy, not because of anything good that we do to try and please God.

TIGER: He gave us the Holy Spirit to help us live right and have life that never ends. The Holy Spirit is sure a lot more powerful than any human being. Not only can He bring Jon to his senses, but He can help him escape Satan's trap of drugs.

AMEN: We need to help Jon understand that God loves him unconditionally and will forgive him. He needs to know Jesus died for him and wants to give him a really full life. The Holy Spirit will give him the strength he needs to seek help so he can kick the habit and be drug free. He can have life that will never end.

VIBES: I feel like praying for Jon right now.

IQ: Great idea! Let's all join together and talk to our Forever Friend, Jesus, about our good friend, Jon.

Service Projects for Substance Abuse

✔ 1. Baby holders can give some individual love to some of the babies born with drug addictions. These babies have many problems—physically and mentally. They are often institutionalized in hospitals or reception centers. As innocent victims of substance abuse, they need more attention than a regular staff can provide. Have a play session with toddlers and hold, feed, bathe, and change babies.

✔ 2. Pet therapy is encouraged in many institutions for their residents. Bring your pets and share them with lonely, developmentally handicapped children and adults who are need of extra attention and stimulation.

✔ 3. Have your class volunteer to talk to kids in a younger class about the dangers of drug use. Encourage your Juniors to see themselves as role models for the younger kids.

✔ 4. Produce a class newspaper giving information about various drugs, alternatives to drug use, how to help a friend, where to go for help, and other insights learned in is unit. Photocopy the newpaper and distribute it to kids at church and school.

Making the Connection . . .

Communicating well with others is one of the most important skills each of us must learn in life. Many of the greatest problems we encounter can be traced back to a lack of clear communication. Misunderstandings, hurt feelings, and regrets over things we wish we had or had *not* said can all be avoided when we learn healthy means of communicating with each other.

Because so many in our society never learn these skills, your Juniors may be growing up without good models of clear communication. As with many of the areas of their lives, they may be taking their cues from TV and movies. Unfortunately, communication styles used to entertain are less than adequate for functioning in real life!

In this unit, you will be teaching your kids how to connect with others through the use of good communication skills. They will learn that communicating is the art of getting a message from one person to another, and that poor communication results when the message we send is different from the one the other person actually receives. Through exploring the dynamics of non-verbal communication, and the practice of good listening skills your students will begin to see that there is much more to communication than just the words they say.

Also during this unit, you will take your kids to Scripture to discover how God communicated with us by sending Jesus. They will see how coming in human form made it possible for Jesus to clearly communicate God's message to us.

✓ Communication With Others Overview

Unit Verse: In these last days he [God] has spoken to us by his Son. Hebrews 1:2a
Unit Affirmation: I CAN LEARN TO COMMUNICATE WELL!

LESSON	TITLE	OBJECTIVE	SCRIPTURE BASE
Lesson #1	Actions Speak as Loud as Words	That your students will understand that we communicate with others through our actions as well as our words.	Hebrews 1: 1-4; 2:1-4
Lesson #2	Straight Talk	That your students will understand thatGod wants us to be completely honest when we communicate with others.	Nehemiah 2:1-8
Lesson #3	Are You Listening to Me?	That your students will develop better listening skills so they will hear beyond the words of others to understand and share the speaker's feelings.	Esther 6:1-13
Lesson #4	Open Up	That your students will reach out to others in God's love and keep lines of communication open with them.	II Samuel 13: 38-14: 3, 12-24, 28, 32, 33

Partners

For the next few weeks your Junior-age child will be part of a group learning about Communication. *Partners* is a planned parent piece to keep you informed of what will be taught during this exciting series.

PREVIEW...
Communication Skills

Learning to communicate well with others is one of life's most important skills. Many of the greatest problems we encounter can be traced back to a lack of clear communication. Misunderstandings, hurt feelings, and regrets over things we wish we had or had *not* said can all be avoided when we learn healthy means of communicating with each other.

It is helpful to remember that good communication is a skill to be learned, and not something we automatically know how to do. As with any skill, learning to communicate well involves learning a few basic principles and then investing lots of time practicing them. As for our children, many today are modeling their communication styles from what they see on TV and movies. Unfortunately, communication styles used to entertain are less than adequate for functioning in real life!

During this unit, your kids will be learning some of the basic skills of good communication, and impressed with the need to be learning and practicing them throughout their lives. Also during this unit, they will explore Scripture to discover how God faced the greatest communication problem of all, and solved it by sending Jesus to communicate with us!

Unit Verse:

In these last days he [God] has spoken to us by his Son. Hebrews 1:2a

Unit Affirmation:

I CAN LEARN TO COMMUNICATE WELL!

PRINCIPLES...
Communication Skills
PRINCIPLE #1:

COMMUNICATION IS THE ART OF GETTING A MESSAGE FROM ONE PERSON TO ANOTHER. As simple as that sounds, often the message the sender intends to communicate is different from the one the other person actually receives. The result is misunderstandings and a poor connection between us and others in our lives. In class, your kids will discover that there are many ways of getting a message across, and that good communication involves much more than just the words we say. They will see that our actions and non-verbal body language are actually more powerful forms of communication than words, and that many confusing messages are sent because our words, actions and body language do not all say the same thing! They will also learn about skills of receiving messages accurately, and focus on active listening as one of those skills.

PRINCIPLE #2:

GOD'S CLEAREST FORM OF COMMUNICATION WITH US IS THROUGH JESUS CHRIST. As difficult as it is for us to get our messages across from human being to human being, think of the problem God has in getting His message across to us! By looking at the Scriptures, your kids will see that God loved us so much He was willing to send His Son to become a human being like us so that He could communicate with us clearly and directly. By studying Jesus' words and actions, they will see that Jesus clearly communicates to us that God loves us totally and completely, and that we can know Him personally through faith in Christ. That's the good news of the Gospel of Jesus Christ!

PRACTICE...

Communication Skills

1. FAMILY PRAYER JOURNAL.

Keeping the lines of communication open with God is the first and most important communication skill you can teach your children. Modeling the value of regular, effective prayer in your own life is one part of teaching kids about prayer. The other is by directly involving them in communicating with God through family prayer times. Keeping a family prayer journal can help make this a special time for your family. All you need is a notebook and a pen! As you pray together, record your requests on one side of a page, reserving the other side for recording God's answers. As time goes by, you will find that reviewing your prayer notebook will become a great source of celebration of God's faithfulness in your lives.

2. PRINCIPLES FOR COMMUNICATING HONESTLY.

In the second lesson of this unit, your kids will learn the following principles for communicating honestly. Make a poster of these principles and post it somewhere where all family members can see it. As a family, talk about the meaning of each one, using the following information:

1. Say what is TRUE. Many times we say things we don't mean or simply are not true. For example, when someone asks us what is wrong and we say "Nothing" when there is, we are not saying what is true. Or, when we call someone a "dumb jerk", we are not saying what is true.

2. Say what you NEED and WANT. Many times we are not honest about what we really need or want from people. For example, if your friend says, "What do you want to do today?" and you say, "I don't care." But then he suggests three things and you won't do any of them because what you really want to do is go to the mall. You were not honest when you said you didn't care. You need to say what you want clearly and honestly.

3. Say it KINDLY and RESPECTFULLY. Sometimes what we say isn't as important as how we say it. It hurts to be yelled at or made fun of or called names. Being honest and clear in our communication means we treat everyone with respect and kindness.

4. Use "I" phrases to say what you FEEL. It's important to tell others what we feel and not blame them for what they did or didn't do. Example: "You made me look like a fool in front of everyone!" is a blaming statement. "I feel embarrassed when you tell my grades to the other kids!" is a straight, clear message that others can hear and understand.

3. HAVE A DAILY "LISTENING TIME" FOR EACH OF YOUR CHILDREN.

You can increase your communication with your children by setting aside a few minutes each day as "listening time" with each of your children. During this time, discipline yourself to listen to your child without lecturing or judging what they are saying. You can use clarifying questions to get at the meaning of what they are saying. ("Are you feeling angry that your teacher picks on you?"; "Exactly what did Jenny say that upset you so much?"; "How are you feeling about getting that award at school today?") You can identify with them by relating similar feelings you have or have had. ("When I was ten, I remember feeling scared about taking math tests, too!"; "I think I felt the same way you are feeling last week when my boss yelled at me for no reason."; "Doesn't it feel good to learn a new skill and find out you really like it?") The point is to give your children an opportunity to have your full attention and to express their deepest feelings without fear of being told they did something wrong or "shouldn't feel that way." It may seem hard to do at first, but you will reap great rewards in the future by keeping the lines of communication open with your kids!

Lesson 1 ✔

Actions Speak as Loud as Words

Aim: That your students will understand that we communicate with others through our actions as well as our words.

Scripture: Hebrews 1:1-4; 2:1-4

Unit Verse: In these last days he [God] has spoken to us by his Son. Hebrews 1:2a

Unit Affirmation: I CAN LEARN TO COMMUNICATE WELL!

 Planning Ahead

1. Photocopy activity sheets (pages 59 and 60)-one for each student.
2. Prepare the Unit Affirmation poster by writing the following across the top of a large poster board: I CAN LEARN TO COM MUNICATE WELL! Under the title, write the numbers 1-4 vertically along the left-hand side.
3. Prepare about six "secret messages" and the category of the message on separate index cards. These will be used for a game in LIVING THE LESSON. Some suggestions for categories are: titles of hymns (example of message "Sweet Hour of Prayer"); Bible personalities (example "Samson"); Bible events (example "the flood"); animals (example "elephant").
4. Prepare stickers for the Unit Verse Activity as described in LIVING THE LESSON.

 1 Setting the Stage (5-10 minutes)

WHAT YOU'LL DO

- Play "Telephone" as an example of poor or unclear communication

WHAT YOU'LL NEED

- Phrases for "Telephone"

 2 Introducing the Issue (20 minutes)

WHAT YOU'LL DO

- Define verbal and non-verbal communication and discuss the need to make our words and actions agree
- Use an activity sheet to brainstorm verbal and non-verbal means of communicating various messages.
- Introduce the Unit Affirmation poster

WHAT YOU'LL NEED

- "Say It With Flowers, or. . . ?" Activity Sheet (page 59)
- Unit Affirmation poster

3 Searching the Scriptures (20 minutes)

WHAT YOU'LL DO

- Use an activity and solve a puzzle to discover ways God communicated with people in Bible times

WHAT YOU'LL NEED

- Bibles
- "When You Care Enough To Send The Very Best" Activity Sheet (page 60)

 4 Living the Lesson (5-10 minutes)

WHAT YOU'LL DO

- Try communicating with others in different ways by playing a charade relay game
- Make stickers that communicate the Unit Verse

WHAT YOU'LL NEED

- Cards with "Secret Messages"
- Adhesive stickers, scissors, markers

✓ Setting the Stage (5-10 minutes)

As your students arrive today, seat them in a circle to play "Telephone." Begin by whispering a "secret message" into someone's ear. That person must pass the message along by whispering it into the ear of the person sitting next to him or her. The only rule is this: They can only whisper the phrase once. They must pass along whatever they heard the first time! Continue passing the phrase around the circle in this manner until it reaches the last person, who will then say it aloud to the whole class. The result will be a perfect example of unclear communication! Here are some phrases that work well:

See the sea shells by the seashore

Cowabunga, Dude!

An apple a day keeps the doctor away

The Lord is my shepherd, I shall not want

Jesus loves me this I know, for the Bible tells me so

What happened to our messages as they were passed around the circle? (They got confused, garbled, miscommunicated.) **Why did this happen?** (Speaker did not speak clearly; listener did not listen well; maybe both.) **At the end of the game, you heard a message that I supposedly started. But what you heard was NOT the message I sent! What happens when what we HEAR is different from what the person actually SAID?** (There are all kinds of misunderstandings and confusion.) **Today we are starting a new unit. For the next four weeks we will be talking about how we communicate with one another, and how we can avoid the kind of miscommunication we experienced in our game just now!**

✓ Introducing the Issue (20 minutes)

What is communication? Allow for responses. **Communication is the ability to get a message from one person to another. On the board, draw two stick figures, labeling one "sender" and the other "receiver." Draw an arrow from sender to receiver, labeling it "message." What are some messages we might want to communicate to each other?** (Anything and everything: "I love you," "Let's be friends," things we are excited about, things we are thinking about, questions we want to ask, etc.) **How do we get these messages across to other people?** The first response we are likely to have to that question is, "We tell them!" But communication involves much more than telling. In fact, non-verbal communication can be much more powerful than verbal! Encourage your kids to think creatively and come up with several ways we let others know what we are thinking and feeling. Possibilities include: facial expressions, physical actions like hugging or hitting, giving gifts, loving deeds, etc. **There are two ways for us to communicate with others. One is called verbal communication, and the other is called non-verbal communication. The first one includes everything we say to others, and the second one is everything we do.**

Distribute copies of the activity sheet, "Say It With Flowers, or. . . ?" (page 59). **Have you ever heard the expression, "Say It With Flowers"? What does it mean?** (Giving someone flowers as a gift communicates the message, "I love you!") **Sometimes, showing people by our actions is a much more powerful way of communicating than just telling them in words. It's easy to say, "I love you," but it takes time and money to actually go out and send flowers. The person who receives the flowers also receives the message, "I love you!" from the sender.** Divide your class into five groups and assign one of the messages on the activity sheet to each group. Give them a few minutes to think of as many ways as they can to communicate their message with words and actions. Ask each group to share its responses with the rest of the class by presenting a little skit as a way to illustrate its answers.

So far, we have made communication sound pretty simple, but many times the message the "receiver" receives is different than the one the "sender" sent! Just like in our opening game, the original message somehow gets lost. Can you think of some things that could happen to keep the receiver from getting the right message? (The sender doesn't say what he really means, the receiver isn't listening, there may be a language barrier, etc.) **Perhaps one of the biggest blocks to good communication is when the sender says one things in words, but acts in a way that gives a whole different message. In other words, the words and actions do not agree.** Illustrate this concept with the following, using exaggerated actions to get your point across.

Say, "I'm so happy to be here today!", using a blah voice and wearing a frown.

Say, "I'm really angry that you told my secret to the whole class," while you are smiling and giggling.

Someone tells you, "I like you and want you to be my friend!" But then she has a birthday party and invites everyone in your class EXCEPT YOU.

Ask the kids to think of more examples.

In order for us to give a clear message, both what we say and do must be giving the same message. When they are different, we get confused

and have lots of misunderstandings.

Display the Unit Affirmation poster, and have the class read it aloud together. The key word in this Affirmation is LEARN. **Good communication is a very important skill that each of us must work very hard to learn. No one is automatically a good communicator. What did we learn today that is an important part of good communication?** (Words and actions must agree.) Write, "by making sure my words and actions agree" on the first line. **As hard as it sometimes is for us to communicate with each other, think of how hard it must be for God to communicate with us! Let's take a look at how God solved His problem of how to get His message across to the people He created!**

Searching the Scriptures (20 minutes)

How many of you know at least a few words of another language? Most kids will think of only a verbal language but emphasize that there are other recognized languages which are non-verbal such as the sign language used by hearing impaired people, sign language used by native Americans during the early history of America, and Braille which is used by the blind. Perhaps you have someone in class who knows one of these languages. Have students share briefly from any of the languages they may know. If you can speak another language, sharing some words or phrases from it would be a good way to introduce this study.

How do you think it would feel to be in a foreign country and not be able to talk with the people who lived there? (It would feel frustrating, frightening, upsetting.) **How do you think you could communicate with people in that kind of situation?** (I'd use hand signals, draw pictures, point a lot.) **God experienced some of these same problems when He wanted to communicate with the people He had created. He wanted them to know more about Himself, to know what He is really like and how to live lives that are pleasing to Him. Let's see what He did to try to tell them these things.** Distribute copies of the activity sheet "When You Care Enough To Send The Very Best" (page 60).

Have someone read the instructions. Students can decode the secret words individually. You may wish to have them work in pairs or small groups on the match-up section as there are a number of passages to look up. Answers for words are: prophets, angels, signs, wonders, miracles, gifts of the Holy Spirit, visions, face to face, dreams. Matching answers are: a-4, b-1, c- 8, d-3, e-3, 4, 5, 6, f-7, g-2, h-5, i-7, 9.

How do you feel when people speak in a language you don't under-

stand? (Left out, wonder if they are talking about you, wish you could understand them.) If your students have not experienced this, another comparison would be watching television or a movie with the sound turned off or listening to an adventure program on the radio and trying to imagine what is going on. **What kinds of problems do you think arose when God used the nine forms of communication mentioned in the activity sheet?** (People were scared of some of them, they misunderstood them, the methods were limited in what they could tell us about God.)

Which method do you think is the most accurate representation of what God was trying to tell us? Have students look up Hebrews 1:1-4 and take turns reading it. **Why is Jesus more reliable than those other ways?** (He spoke our language, He is the exact copy of God's nature, His actions reinforced what He said, He could explain things and answer questions.) **One of the names the Bible uses for Jesus is "the Word." Jesus was God's Word to us in human form.**

If Jesus is easier to understand than these other methods of communication, how can we respond to what He has said and done? Let's turn to Hebrews 2:1-4 to find the answer. Have students take turns reading this passage. (Realize Jesus' communications are more important, pay more attention to it, follow His example.)

Can you think of some examples where an action of Jesus agreed with something He taught us about God or how we should live to please God? Some examples are: "God loves sinners" and Jesus ate with sinners and tax collectors at the home of Zacchaeus; "God's house is to be used for prayer and worship only" and Jesus drove the merchants out of the temple; "God loves people who are outcasts from society" and Jesus touched and healed the leper; "We should forgive each other" and Jesus forgave Peter for denying Him.

Jesus didn't say one thing and do another. His actions and words matched.

☑ Living the Lesson (5-10 minutes)

Today we're going to play a relay game to see just how important our actions really are. Divide your class into two teams. Explain that in this game one member from each team will be given a secret message and its category. These two "messengers" can tell the category only and then must communicate the message to their own team without speaking. They can draw, use sign language, or act it out. When the team guesses the right answer, another member will go get a message which he or she must also communicate to the team. The game will continue in this manner until all messages have been

guessed. The first team to get all the messages wins. Have pencils and paper ready for those who want to draw their messages. Give the teams a chance to choose their "messengers." On your signal, the first messengers will race to you and get their message.

How easy was it to understand the messages without words? (Most kids will agree it was rather difficult.) **Words are important when you want to be sure that your message is understood aren't they? That's why God sent the "Word," Jesus to communicate with us.** Have students turn to the Unit Verse, Hebrews 1:2a, and read it together. Encourage the students to understand that God loves them so much that He wants them to be able to really understand what He is like. He wants them to comprehend the wonderful plans He has for them and how they can have the most satisfying life of all. In order to avoid any misunderstandings, He sent someone who was the exact copy of His nature. That someone is Jesus. By listening to what Jesus said and seeing how He acted, we get a picture of God's loving nature. Because Jesus is God, we need to obey the things He told us and follow His example. And we need to be sure our own words and actions agree.

Before class, make adhesive stickers for the Unit Verse activity. Draw a number of two-inch circles on a sheet of typing paper, leaving room around the circles to cut them apart. Make enough circles for at least one per student. Mix equal amounts of Elmer's or LePage's Mucilage and water together in a small paper cup. Use a paintbrush to apply the glue mixture to the back of the sticker page. Let the page dry completely, glue side up. When dry, cut the stickers apart.

Distribute the adhesive stickers, markers, and scissors. **You can now create a sticker, using words, and symbols that illustrate our new Unit Verse.** Allow students to design, color, and cut out their stickers. **These stickers are self-adhesive. When you want to use them, dampen the back of them with a lightly wet sponge or brush.**

Close class with a great non-verbal communication—a group hug.

Say It With Flowers Or...?

How many ways can you think of to communicate the following messages?

I LOVE YOU!

With words:_____

_____

With actions: _____

_____

I'M ANGRY!

With words:_____

_____

With actions:_____

_____

I WANT TO BE YOUR FRIEND!

With words:_____

_____

With actions:_____

_____

I'M FRIGHTENED!

With words:_____

_____

With actions:_____

_____

GOD LOVES YOU!

With words:_____

_____

With actions:_____

_____

When You Care Enough to Send the Very Best

Discover methods God used to communicate with people in the past.
Decode the words in column one. Look up the passages listed in column two that tell us of ways God communicated with people. Write the number of the method by its match. Two verses have more than one method.

Code: A C D E F G H I J L M N O P R S T U V W Y

1. ☺ ☎ ♥ ✎ ★ ♠ ❦ ▲
   _ _ _ _ _ _ _ _

2. ✡ ■ ✳ ♠ ● ▲
   _ _ _ _ _ _

3. ▲ ☆ ✳ ■ ▲
   _ _ _ _ _

4. ☽ ♥ ■ ⇔ ♠ ☎ ▲
   _ _ _ _ _ _ _

5. ✈ ☆ ☎ ✡ ✤ ● ♠ ▲
   _ _ _ _ _ _ _ _

6. ✳ ☆ ✦ ❦ ▲   ♥ ✦   ❦ ★ ♠   ★ ♥ ● ✌   ▲ ✎ ☆ ☎ ☆ ❦
   _ _ _ _ _   _ _   _ _ _   _ _ _ _   _ _ _ _ _ _

7. ❖ ☆ ▲ ☆ ♥ ■ ▲
   _ _ _ _ _ _ _

8. ✦ ✡ ✤ ♠   ❦ ♥   ✦ ✡ ✤ ♠
   _ _ _ _   _ _   _ _ _ _

9. ⇔ ☎ ♠ ✡ ✈ ▲
   _ _ _ _ _ _

__ a. Exodus 34:10

__ b. James 5:10

__ c. Numbers 12:8

__ d. Exodus 4:9

__ e. Hebrews 2:4

__ f. Ezekiel 8:3

__ g. Luke 2:15

__ h. Acts 19:11

__ i. Numbers 12:6

God cares for us so much that He wants us to be able to really understand Him and how He wants us to live. So He sent the very best communication of all. Look up Hebrews 1:1, 2 to find out what God sent. Write it on the line below.

_____

Lesson 2

Straight Talk

Aim: That your students will understand that God wants us to be completely honest when we communicate with others.

Scripture: Nehemiah 2:1-8

Unit Verse: In these last days he [God] has spoken to us by his Son. Hebrews 1:2a

Unit Affirmation: I CAN LEARN TO COMMUNICATE WELL!

 **Planning Ahead**

1. Photocopy activity sheets (pages 67 and 68)-one for each student.
2. Prepare role-play cards as described in LIVING THE LESSON.

1 Setting the Stage (5-10 minutes)

WHAT YOU'LL DO

- Play "Simon Says" as an illustration of saying one thing but meaning another

WHAT YOU'LL NEED

- Phrases or commands to use in "Simon Says"

2 Introducing the Issue (20 minutes)

WHAT YOU'LL DO

- Use an activity sheet to talk about four guidelines for communicating honestly
- Add a phrase to the Unit Affirmation poster

WHAT YOU'LL NEED

- "Give It To Me Straight!" Activity Sheet (page 67)
- Unit Affirmation poster

3 Searching the Scriptures (20 minutes)

WHAT YOU'LL DO

- Use an activity sheet and dramatize a story to find out how a king's cupbearer communicated honestly with the king

WHAT YOU'LL NEED

- Bibles
- "Quantum Leap Into Honesty" Activity Sheet (page 68)

4 Living the Lesson (5-10 minutes)

WHAT YOU'LL DO

- Use role-plays to practice ways of communicating honestly
- Create a design for a T-shirt which will communicate today's focus from the Unit Verse, honesty.

WHAT YOU'LL NEED

- Three role-play cards
- Paper and drawing supplies-one for each student

✓ Setting the Stage (5-10 minutes)

As your students arrive today, involve them in playing "Simon Says" as a way to illustrate today's lesson theme. To play, stand everyone in a circle. Then issue a series of commands, prefaced with the phrase, "Simon Says. . . ." The group must follow your command. Every so often, you will give a command without the initial phrase, "Simon Says. . . ." When that happens, participants are not to do the command. Anyone who does it anyway is "caught" and eliminated from the circle. To be successful, you will have to keep it moving quickly. You might add some variety by inviting various students to be the leader. Examples of commands: "Simon Says hop on one foot," "Simon Says rub your tummy and pat your head at the same time," "Simon Says run in place," "Simon Says shake hands with your neighbor," "Turn around in a circle."

After a few minutes of play, stop the game. **Why did some of you get "caught" in this game?** (It's easy to get so involved in following the directions, we stop listening to the first part.) **When we play long enough and go fast enough, it can get very confusing to follow all the directions. That's because in reality I am saying one thing to you, but meaning something entirely different! I am tricking you with my words!**

✓ Introducing the Issue (20 minutes)

When we communicate with others, it is very important that we learn to say what we really mean. When our words say one thing, but what we really mean is something altogether different, we confuse the other person and leave him or her trying to figure out what is going on. Use the following illustrations to reinforce this point:

1. You walk into a room and see your best friend looking sad and depressed. You say, "Hey, what's wrong?" Your friend replies, "Nothing." Your friend's words say one thing, but they mean something else. Now you are confused, and don't know how to figure out what is wrong or how to help.

2. You are sitting in the kitchen when your Mom comes in and yells, "Why didn't you hang up your coat? I asked you this morning and you didn't do it! Now I have to pick up after you, and that's not fair!" You think she is overreacting, and you don't know why she is so mad at you for such a little thing. You wonder, "What's going on?"

3. You are very angry at your friend for telling the other kids that you got a "D" on your math test. You felt embarrassed because they knew. Your friend

comes up to you and says, "Hey, I guess I shouldn't have told the other kids about your math test, huh?" You look at her coldly and say, "It's no big deal," and walk away.

Have you ever heard the expression, "Just say it straight out!" or, "Be straight with me, man!" What do you think that means? (Be honest; say what is really on your mind; don't beat around the bush; say what you really mean.) **If we want to be good communicators, we must learn to say what we really mean in straight, clear messages**. Distribute copies of the activity sheet, "Give It To Me Straight," (page 67) and look at it together. Give a few minutes for the kids to unscramble the words to complete the four rules. Then talk about each one:

1. Say what is TRUE. Many times we say things we don't mean or simply are not true. For example, when someone asks us what is wrong and we say "Nothing" when there is, we are not saying what is true. Or, when we call someone a "dumb jerk", we are not saying what is true.

2. Say what you NEED and WANT. Many times we are not honest about what we really need or want from people. For example, if your friend says, "What do you want to do today?" and you say, "I don't care." But then he suggests three things and you won't do any of them because what you really want to do is go to the Mall. You were not honest when you said you didn't care. You need to say what you want clearly and honestly.

3. Say it KINDLY and RESPECTFULLY. Sometimes what we say isn't as important as how we say it. It hurts to be yelled at or made fun of or called names. Being honest and clear in our communication means we treat everyone with respect and kindness.

4. Use "I" phrases to say what you FEEL. It's important to tell others what we feel and not blame them for what they did or didn't do. Example: "You made me look like a fool in front of everyone!" is a blaming statement. "I feel embarrassed when you tell my grades to the other kids!" is a straight, clear message that others can hear and understand.

Now let's put these rules to work by helping the kids in the cartoons change their statements to clear, straight honest ones. How could we rewrite the first one? (I feel angry when you take my things without asking me first! I want you to stay out of my room unless I am there with you.) **The second one?** (I feel frustrated that you have chosen the TV programs the last three nights. I would like to choose the program tonight.) **The last one?** (I feel lonely when Dad has to work so many nights, and I miss him. I need him to spend some extra time with me real soon!)

Display the Unit Affirmation poster, and read it aloud together. Ask kids to think of a phrase that they could add this week. Possibilities might be, "by

being honest with others," or "by saying what we really mean." **It's not always easy to be completely honest when we communicate with others; in fact, sometimes it is very hard! But it is something we can practice and learn to do well. Now let's look at a person in the Bible who learned about communicating honestly.**

 # Searching the Scriptures (20 minutes)

One of the reasons people aren't honest when they communicate is because they are afraid of what others may think. People in Bible times felt the same way. Let's see what happened when one man took control of his fears and told the truth.

Introduce the activity sheet by explaining "Quantum Leap" as follows: During an experiment about time something strange happens and Dr. Scram Beckett is zapped back in time. Directed there by an authoritative power source he finds himself sent to different periods of history. In each situation Scram has been sent back to replace someone of that time period and to help out people involved in a problem. Instead of appearing like a stranger when other people see or hear him, he looks and sounds like the person he has been sent to replace. An assistant, Pal, is there to help Scram. He is invisible and inaudible to everyone but Scram. Another helper, Ziggy, is a master computer that provides historical information needed to help Scram adjust to his new situation.

Distribute copies of the activity sheet "Quantum Leap Into Honesty" (page 68). You will need people to take the parts of Scram, the king, Pal, and a soldier.

If your kids enjoy drama and you have a longer class period, act out the play. You can use cardboard crowns, a cup, pitcher, and a pocket calculator. Because Pal is invisible to all but Scram, the other characters freeze in place when these two converse.

How did Nehemiah feel about the troubles his people were having back in Judah? (He felt very sad.) Point out that he felt so sad that he prayed about it for four months, wanted to help them, and was courageous enough to talk to the king about it. **When we don't communicate honestly with others, they have to guess at what we are feeling or thinking about. This frequently leads to misunderstandings.**

How did Nehemiah express those feelings to the king? (He expressed them respectfully, honestly, sincerely.) Emphasize that how you say things is as important as what you say. Your attitude has a lot to do with how people respond to you. Point out that when Nehemiah communicated his feeling genuinely, the king realized how much the rebuilding of Jerusalem meant to his favorite servant.

Nehemiah went on to describe what the problem was. This took away accusations or name-calling and allowed the king to concentrate on the problem. It made him feel that Nehemiah had confidence in him and really needed his help. **How did the king respond to Nehemiah?** (He asked what Nehemiah wanted.) **The king was actually asking what Nehemiah wanted him to do about the problem. What did Nehemiah say?** (He asked to be sent to rebuild the city, that he needed letters for safe travel, timber for building.) **Nehemiah gave the king information as to what could be done and how to do it. He spoke to what was best in the king and opened the way for his master to act responsibly.**

How did the king respond to Nehemiah's requests? (He granted all of them.) This complete fulfillment of Nehemiah's petition reveals the reputation for honesty that this man of God had. In those days many kings were assassinated by poisoning. The king's life was literally in his cupbearer's hands. He knew his servant was trustworthy. **Nehemiah was completely truthful in words and actions. If he said he needed certain things or would be back by a specific time, you could depend upon him. Can people depend upon you to communicate with them honestly?**

Living the Lesson (5-10 minutes)

Before class write three role-play situations on index cards. They are:

1. April and Beth are good friends. Jenny told April about the disappearance of Kristen's purse yesterday. "Kristen thinks she left it in the music room. Beth was the last one out of the room so Kristen said she must have stolen it."

2. Jim got a track award. He rushed home to tell his mom. He had just started to tell all about it when his little brother, Michael, burst into the kitchen. Michael was angry with his friend and began to complain about him to Mom.

3. Rhonda asked to borrow her brother Ken's tape cassette for a party. A week later when Ken wanted to play it, he couldn't locate it. He finally found it at the bottom of Rhonda's sweater drawer. The tape was all tangled and broken.

Now you're going to have an opportunity to deal with some of the types of problems you may encounter in real life. By learning how to handle them in class, you will be better prepared to face them when you communicate with others. Assign three groups of students to role-play the situations you prepared before class. Hand each group a problem card. Allow

them a few minutes to plan the drama. Make your class a warm, safe place where kids can feel secure about sharing their emotions and imperfect tries. Be sure to affirm those who risk getting involved. If you have a small class, students may have to take part in more than one role-play.

Encourage all students to participate. Those who do not act in role-plays are responsible for making observations and thinking of alternatives to those being presented. If students have difficulty in their roles, either play one part yourself or send in an additional person to help out. End the role-play when the roles have been effectively presented. Ending them at a "what happens next?" point helps promote discussion.

> **OPTIONAL:** If students feel comfortable about it, videotape these role-plays. You can replay them and stop the action for discussion questions.

Ask the actors how they felt about their roles and responses. Discuss the drama as a group. **What do you think the characters were feeling? Why do you think they acted the way they did? What makes people act that way sometimes? Did the characters say what is true or resort to name calling and finger-pointing? Did the characters follow the biblical principles on communicating honestly?**

Ask someone to read Hebrews 1:2a. **God sent His Son, Jesus, to communicate honestly with us. Jesus spoke the truth. When people honestly sought Him, He stated their problems and focused attention on their sins, but did not resort to name calling. He sincerely expressed His Father's feelings, correcting wrong impressions people had of God. He told people what God and they could do to eliminate their problems. Jesus is the true reflection of God's character. By both actions and words He earned the right to say, "I am the truth."**

Everybody loves to read T-shirts. They are like walking billboards, telling people what we think and feel. Hand out paper and drawing supplies. Have kids draw a simple T-shirt shape on the paper. See illustration.

Create a design about talking straight for a T-shirt you would like to wear. You can use words, pictures, or a combination of both.

Close class with prayer, asking God to help you to be honest in all your communications with each other.

Give It to Me Straight!

✔

Unscramble the words below to discover four important rules for communicating honestly. Then use the rules to help each child give a straight, clear message.

RULE #1: Say what is _____.

ETUR

RULE #2: Say what you _____ or _____.

EDEN   TWNA

RULE #3: Say it _____ and _____.

YLNIDK   YLRPCSEFLUTE

RULE #4: Use "I" phrases to say what you _____.

LEEF

You clumsy idiot! You broke my airplane! Won't you ever learn to stay out of my stuff?!

I feel _____!
I want _____.

How come you always get to choose what we watch on TV and I never get to?

I feel _____.
I would like _____.

What do you mean Dad has to work again tonight? He loves his dumb old job more than me!

I feel _____.
I need _____.

Quantum Leap Into Honesty

(King Artaxerxes and the Queen are seated at a table eating with a number of nobles. The king is holding up his cup. A group of servants and soldiers stand in attendance. Scram stands with a pitcher next to the king.)

KING: Are you going to fill my cup, Nehemiah? I am waiting.

SCRAM: I'm sorry sir, uh, your majesty. I'll fill it immediately. (fills cup, looks around, confused)

PAL: (appears out of crowd, all but Pal and Scram freeze) Better watch it, Scram. Servants to King Artaxerxes of Persia have lost their heads for inattention.

SCRAM: Pal, you're just in time. So that's where I am. But WHO am I? What am I doing with this pitcher?

PAL: (consulting calculator in hand) Your name is Nehemiah and you're the cupbearer to the king. It's your job to see that no one puts poison in the king's drink. You are a Jew and your people were brought here as captives. Ziggy says this man, Nehemiah, found out that his countrymen back in Judah are in a lot of trouble and he-you-has been all broken up about it. He's been praying to God for four months to help him talk to the king about it and get him to help the Jews rebuild their city, Jerusalem.

SCRAM: (looks sad) Four months? The poor guy! But if I'm just a servant? (King leans toward Scram)

KING: Why do you look so sad? You don't seem sick. (nobles and servants are shocked and start to murmur among themselves)

PAL: Now you've done it, Scram! The king can execute anyone who annoys him by showing sorrow. (a soldier steps forward)

SOLDIER: Shall I arrest him, your majesty? (the king shakes his head and waves him aside; crowd looks surprised)

KING: Let him speak. (all but Pal and Scram freeze)

SCRAM: What shall I say, Pal? I'm really scared!

PAL: This may be the opportunity Nehemiah's been waiting for, Scram. This guy really trusts you. Why not just be honest? (Pal steps to side; Scram sets down pitcher, steps in front of King and bows; crowd strains to listen)

PAL: May you live forever, O King! I'm sad because the city of Jerusalem, where my ancestors are buried is in ruins.

KING: What do you want?

SCRAM: (looks toward heaven and says very quietly) Help me, God. (takes deep breath and addresses King) If you are willing and if I have pleased you, send me to Jerusalem. Let me rebuild the city. (Queen taps King on arm and whispers in his ear; King nods and looks at Scram)

KING: How long will your trip take? When would you get back? (Pal steps over to Scram; all others freeze)

PAL: I can't believe it, Scram. He's really going to send you to Jerusalem!

SCRAM: I guess it was being completely honest with him that did it. That plus lots of prayer and God's help. (Pal steps aside; Scram turns to King) If you are willing, I need. . . (Pal steps forward and speaks to audience; everyone else freezes; Pal looks at calculator)

PAL: Ziggy says you'll do OK, Nehemiah. The wall will get built in record time, the Jews will return to worship the Lord. You'll even get to be governor of Judah. Communicating honestly sure paid off!

Are You Listening to Me?

Aim: That your students will develop better listening skills so they will hear beyond the words of others to understand and share the speaker's feelings.

Scripture: Esther 6:1-13

Unit Verse: In these last days he [God] has spoken to us by his Son. Hebrews 1:2a

Unit Affirmation: I CAN LEARN TO COMMUNICATE WELL!

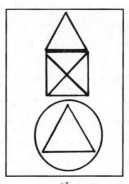 

#1   #2

 Planning Ahead

1. Photocopy activity sheets (pages 75 and 76)-one for each student.
2. Copy the following shapes onto half sheets of paper. Make enough of each so that half of your class gets #1, and the other half gets #2.
3. Write and cover pronunciation helps and pre-record student instructions as described in SEARCHING THE SCRIPTURES.

1 Setting the Stage (5-10 minutes)

WHAT YOU'LL DO

- Draw a shape by listening to verbal commands from a partner.

WHAT YOU'LL NEED

- Shapes copied unto paper

2 Introducing the Issue (20 minutes)

WHAT YOU'LL DO

- Brainstorm characteristics of good listeners
- Use an activity sheet to identify good listening skills
- Add a phrase to the Unit Affirmation poster

WHAT YOU'LL NEED

- "To Hear, or Not To Hear", Activity Sheet (page 75)
- Unit Affirmation poster

3 Searching the Scriptures (20 minutes)

WHAT YOU'LL DO

- Listen for directions in order to discover what happened when an egotistical man heard only what he wanted to and jumped to a hasty conclusion
- Use an activity sheet to write a radio commercial for God's spokesman, Jesus

WHAT YOU'LL NEED

- Chalk and chalkboard or marker and large sheet of paper
- Tape recorder with pre-recorded instructions
- "For Our Listening Audience", Activity Sheet (page 76)
- Bibles

4 Living the Lesson (5-10 minutes)

WHAT YOU'LL DO

- Practice listening skills for verbal and non-verbal communi cations from others

WHAT YOU'LL NEED

- Paper and pencils

 # Setting the Stage (5-10 minutes)

As your students arrive today, put them in pairs and have them try this listening activity. Each pair sits back to back. Give one person a blank paper and a pencil, and the other one a copy of one of the shapes you prepared earlier (See PLANNING AHEAD). Instruct those holding the shapes that they are the "senders" and their task is to help their partners reproduce the same shape on their papers, without ever seeing it! They will do this by telling their partner how to draw it. Those who will be drawing are the "receivers" and they will have to listen very carefully in order to draw the shape correctly. Receivers may not ask any questions during the drawing time. Now give the pairs time to complete their drawings.

When they are finished, let the partners compare the shapes. Recognize the ones that came closest, and those that weren't even close. **What was the hardest part about being the "sender"?** Allow for responses. **What was the hardest part about being the "receiver"?** Allow for responses. **Why do you think the pictures did not match exactly?** (Differences in perception between what the "sender" said and what the "receiver" heard.) **This game shows us that listening well is not always as easy as it sounds! There is a real art to being a good listener, and we will talk about that today.**

If time allows, repeat the exercise allowing the partners to switch roles. Use the second set of shapes you prepared earlier.

Introducing the Issue (20 minutes)

Many kids say that they want to be listened to more often. What do you think they mean by that? Kids often feel that their parents and other adults do not see or hear them much of the time. They know instinctively when they are being tolerated and when they are really being heard. **What is the difference between someone hearing you talk and really listening to you?** (People can hear your words but they don't "sink in". They never understand what you are really saying and feeling.) **How do you know when someone is really listening to you?** Write the responses on the board, guiding your students to think of as many characteristics of good listening as they can. Add some items yourself, so that when your list is complete it contains all of the following. Spend a few minutes discussing each one.

GOOD LISTENERS. . .
1) . . . GIVE THEIR FULL ATTENTION TO THE PERSON SPEAKING. They

aren't doing something else or thinking about something else. The best way to show we are really listening is by eye contact. Looking directly into someone's eyes while he or she is talking says we aren't busy with anything else.

2) . . . ASK QUESTIONS ABOUT WHAT THE SPEAKER IS SAYING. When they feel confused by something the speaker said, or they want to know more, good listeners ask for clarification.

3) . . . CHECK FOR UNDERSTANDING. They may say something like, "Let me see if I understand what you are saying," or, "You mean. . . " and then repeat what they heard.

4) . . . TRY TO FEEL WHAT THE OTHER PERSON IS FEELING. Good listeners don't make fun of the speaker or call him or her names. Instead, they try to be sympathetic and understand what the other person must feel like right now.

5) . . . READ BETWEEN THE LINES. This is the tricky part of listening. It means that we try to figure out what the person means that he or she maybe hasn't said yet. We get clues by looking at the way the person is sitting or standing or the facial expression. For instance, if a friend looks very sad when he tells you his grandparents left after visiting for a week, you might read between the lines and say, "You are going to miss them a lot, aren't you?" But, if he looks happy when he says they left, you might read between the lines and say, "I'll bet it will seem good to get your room back again, won't it?"

Now let's see if we can recognize some good listening skills. Distribute copies of the activity sheet, "To Hear or Not to Hear," (page 75), and give students a few minutes to work through it. **Which pictures showed good listening skills?** (#3 - The listener is giving his full attention; #4 - This friend is reading between the lines and figuring out that something is wrong with his friend even if he says there isn't; #6 - Checking for understanding and asking questions to clarify meaning.) **What's the problem with the others?** (#1 - Not giving full attention to the speaker; #2 and #5 - Not feeling what the other person is feeling.) **How could each of these kids respond in ways that would help good listening?** (#1 - Stop playing with the airplane and look at the speaker; #2 - Could say something like, "I'm sorry you are feeling so badly about your math test. You must feel disappointed!"; #5 - Could say, "Water can be dangerous especially when you're afraid of it. Let's go together to tell the teacher.")

Display the Unit Affirmation poster. Read the Affirmation together aloud, and review each of the previous statements. **What phrase can we add to our poster from today's lesson?** Possibilities might include, "by REALLY listening to others," or "by following the rules of being a good listener." Choose one phrase and write it on the third line. **Just like all the other things we've learned about communication, being a good listener is something we**

have to practice to learn to do well. Unfortunately, many people never learn to be good listeners. Now let's look at a story in the Bible that shows a man who wasn't a very good listener!

 # Searching the Scriptures (20 minutes)

Before class write these instructions on the chalkboard or a large sheet of paper: "Pronunciation helps; Mordecai—MOR-duh- kye; Bigthana—big-THANE-uh; Teresh—TEE-resh; Haman—HAY-mun." Keep these instructions covered until time for the Bible study. Pre-record the rest of the instructions on tape using a clear, strong voice: 1. Turn to Esther 6:1-13 in your Bibles; 2. Take turns reading this passage. Beginning with the person on the teacher's right, each student will read one verse aloud until all thirteen verses are read.

When you record, leave some space between directions so they can be replayed.

Reveal the written helps and play the tape. Look at the person on your right expectantly and smile to encourage him or her. Use non-verbal teaching methods such as pointing at the pronunciation helps and students, re-playing the tape, smiles, nods, etc.; but don't speak to students until they have finished reading the story.

How did you feel about having to follow directions this way? Answers will vary. Most students will say it was harder to do or more confusing than normal. **Good listening means we have to concentrate. In our story today which man was the better listener?** Explain that the king was the better listener because he knew what was read and realized that Mordecai had saved his life.

Why do you think Haman was such a bad listener? (He was thinking of what he was going to ask the king, was self-centered, heard only what he wanted to hear.) **Haman was an egotistical man who was consumed with hatred for Mordecai. All his thoughts centered on himself and those things which directly affected him. Nothing else mattered. Why do you think Haman answered the king as he did in verses 7-9?** Haman was so vain that he thought everyone must be thinking about how wonderful he was. Only the night before, he had been bragging to everyone how popular and respected he was because he was invited to Queen Esther's banquet. Now he told the king the things he wanted someone to do for himself.

To be a good listener you have to put everything aside and give your undivided attention to the person who is speaking. Point out that Haman heard the words that the king spoke, but not the manner in which he spoke them. Good listeners reach beyond the words that are said and understand the meaning of the message and the feelings of the speaker. Body language can give us good clues.

What happened because Haman didn't really listen to the king? (He had to honor and serve his arch-enemy, Mordecai.) **The Bible has some very funny and ironic incidents to share with us. This story is one of them. How do you think Haman felt about having to honor Mordecai publicly?** (He felt humiliated, embarrassed, angry, stupid.) **Have you ever had a time when you wished you had listened better to something? What happened?** Encourage kids to share incidents with the class. By sharing something yourself, you will help students to identify with you and be more open.

Have students look up the Unit Verse in Hebrews 1:2a and repeat it together. **Our Unit Verse talks about God speaking to us. Have you considered listening to God? If we are to be good listeners, we must also learn to hear God. How can we hear God's voice?** (When we read the Bible, hear a sermon, listen to hymns and songs, listen to Sunday school teachers and parents.) **What prevents us from hearing God?** (When we are thinking about something else, not paying attention.) **Do you think there are times when people don't want to hear what God has to say? If so, why not?** (Because they don't want to obey Him or do something He might ask them to do.)

Our verse says that God spoke through His Son, Jesus. Why then do you think God sent Jesus to be His "Word"? Explain that it is harder to ignore or misunderstand actions than mere words. **Jesus not only spoke God's words, but He lived the way God wants us to live. When people saw Jesus heal the sick, reach out to the poor and neglected outcasts, and humbly wash the feet of His followers, they couldn't ignore Him. The people who were waiting and looking for God to speak to them saw and heard God's love in Jesus. Those who didn't want to hear God purposely closed their ears like naughty children. Perhaps that is why Jesus often said, "He who has ears to hear, let him hear." We need to lay everything else aside and focus our attention on Jesus' words and actions to be able to hear God's voice clearly.**

Distribute copies of the activity sheet, "For Our Listening Audience," (page 76) and ask someone to read the directions aloud. Kids will write a radio commercial that promotes Jesus as God's spokesman. It should bring out some of the things that have been discussed in this and previous lessons. Emphasize that the audience will be only listening. No visuals can be used. They will need to paint a verbal picture of Jesus. Have your students read their commercials when they have completed them.

Lesson 3

✓ Living the Lesson (5-10 minutes)

Some of your students may have hesitated to read their ads out loud to their classmates. **Many times we hesitate to talk about things because we are afraid others will make fun of us, reject us, or not take us seriously. Good listening is a skill that all of us need to learn and practice daily. Today you're going to be "private ears." No, I didn't make a mistake and mean private eyes. Someone has said that what people need are "Private Ears" who will just listen and accept them.** Explain that to be private ears, students will need to practice the good methods they talked about in the first part of the lesson. Briefly review these techniques.

Divide your class into small groups of two or three people. Have students share briefly within their groups some incident from this past week. It can be either good or bad. After everyone in the group has shared, distribute paper and pencils. Ask kids to list as many details as they can remember. **What kind of listeners were you? Were you a good observer of body language, feelings, and words? Or were you involved in thinking about what you were going to say?** Probably most of them will admit they didn't listen as well as they could have. Encourage them to understand that like other skills, listening can, and will, improve with practice.

Close the class by having students pray sentence prayers asking God to help them become better listeners.

To Hear or Not to Hear

Look at each picture and decide if it shows good or bad listening skills. Below each one, describe what is being done right or wrong.

1. _____

2. _____

3. _____

4. _____

5. _____

6. _____

✓ For Our Listening Audience...

You are a writer for a large radio station. You have just been asked to write a commercial for Jesus. Your job is to communicate to listeners that God speaks to people through His Son, Jesus. What will you write?

_____
_____
_____
_____
_____
_____
_____
_____
_____
_____
_____
_____
_____
_____
_____
_____
_____
_____
_____

Open Up

Aim: That your students will reach out to others in God's love and keep lines of communication open with them.

Scripture: II Samuel 13:38-14:3, 12-24, 28, 32, 33

Unit Verse: In these last days he [God] has spoken to us by his Son. Hebrews 1:2a

Unit Affirmation: I CAN LEARN TO COMMUNICATE WELL!

 Planning Ahead

1. Photocopy activity sheets (pages 83 and 84)–one for each student.
2. Locate a minimum of 10 building blocks for the object lesson during INTRODUCING THE ISSUE. These need to be fairly large blocks, like the ones used with preschoolers. If you do not have access to blocks, make some with empty half gallon milk cartons. Cut off the tops and wrap the carton with colored paper or contact paper.

1 Setting the Stage (5-10 minutes)

WHAT YOU'LL DO

- Play "Sculptionary" as a way to illustrate barriers to communication

WHAT YOU'LL NEED

- A container of Play Doh or modeling clay for every 3-4 students

2 Introducing the Issue (20 minutes)

WHAT YOU'LL DO

- See an object lesson to discover how barriers to communication separate us from others
- Use an activity sheet to role play blocked and open communication styles
- Complete the Unit Affirmation poster

WHAT YOU'LL NEED

- Building blocks, tape, and slips of paper cut to a size that will fit on the front of the blocks
- "Am I Making Myself Perfectly Clear?", Activity Sheet (page 83)
- Unit Affirmation poster

3 Searching the Scriptures (20 minutes)

WHAT YOU'LL DO

- Use an activity to find out the problems that a lack of communication caused a father and his son

WHAT YOU'LL NEED

- Bibles
- "The Complicated Case Of The Closed Communication", Activity Sheet (page 84)

4 Living the Lesson (5-10 minutes)

WHAT YOU'LL DO

- Brainstorm ways to keep lines of communication open
- Write a letter to someone with whom you need to maintain an open communication

WHAT YOU'LL NEED

- Paper and pencils

 Setting the Stage (5-10 minutes)

As your students arrive today, prepare to play "Sculptionary" by dividing them into teams of three to four players and giving each team a container of Play-Doh or clay. To play, ask one person from each team to come forward and read a word that you will show them. They must then return to their team and use the Play-Doh to make a sculpture depicting that word. They can only use the Play-Doh, they may not use words, sounds, or actions to communicate their word. The first team that correctly guesses the word is awarded 10 points. Repeat the process, having team members take turns being the sculptor. Possible words to use: Fence, Tree, House, Flag, Airplane, etc.

How did it feel to be the one to communicate to your teammates by making a sculpture? Allow for responses. **How did it feel to be the ones trying to figure out what the sculptor was trying to say?** Allow for responses. **In this game we experienced some barriers in communicating the meaning of a word. What were some of those barriers?** (Can't use the most obvious forms of communication, poor artist skills of the sculptor, poor perception skills of the teammates; etc.)

Introducing the Issue (20 minutes)

Place the building blocks (See PLANNING AHEAD.) in the middle of your table, or seat the class in a circle on the floor with the blocks in the middle. Give everyone a slip of paper and a pencil. **For the past few weeks we have been talking about learning good communication skills. So far, we've said that communication is getting a message across to another person. What happens when we are able to communicate effectively with others?** (We feel connected, we build good friendships, we get along better with our parents and other family members, etc.) **Communication is the means by which we build the most important relationships in our lives. When the communication lines are open, we have good relationships. But as we have already seen, sometimes we don't use good communication skills. What happens then?** (We get confused, we have misunderstandings, we don't get our needs met, etc.) **Today we want to talk about some of the things that make communicating with each other difficult, and that even shut down communication altogether. What do you think some of those things are?** Encourage your kids to think back over the past three weeks and remember what they have learned. Barriers to good communication are simply the opposite of healthy communication skills.

As they mention significant barriers, ask someone to write that item on a slip of paper and then tape it to one of the blocks. As this is done, they can stack their blocks in the middle of the table or circle to create a wall. Obviously, the more blocks you use, the more effective this visual will be, so feel free to add some "blank" blocks periodically to help build up the wall. Barriers that could be listed include: not listening, put downs, name calling, anger, pride (too proud to say "I'm sorry"), revenge (you called me a name so I'll get even and won't talk to you anymore), making fun of the other's feelings, nagging, complaining, whining, etc.

Whenever we communicate in one of these ways, it is like we are building a wall between us and the other people in our lives. What happens when we do that? (We feel hurt or guilty, we lose a friend, we might get punished by parents, etc.) **Using good communication skills is the only way we can destroy these barriers between us and others.**

Distribute copies of the activity sheet, "Am I Making Myself Perfectly Clear?" (page 83). Ask for a volunteer to read the first scenario, and then let the class identify what happened to close communication in that situation. Do the same for the second scenario. (Barriers are: #1 - Both boys are caught in blaming the other person, saying something that isn't true, and disregarding the others' feelings. #2 - Mom was not sensitive to her daughter's feelings of being tired and wanting to watch the end of the TV show. Angela reacted in anger and did not use "I" statements to communicate what she was feeling and needed.)

Now divide your class into two groups and assign one of the scenarios to each. Give each group a few minutes to prepare a different ending to its story, illustrating the use of good communication skills. Circulate between the groups as they work, giving suggestions if needed. (Examples: #1 - Eric could read between the lines and use an "I" statement to communicate his feelings, "I guess you're disappointed that we lost the game. So am I! I felt really bad that I couldn't be there. But it's not true that it's all my fault. I couldn't help being sick, and we might have lost anyway!" #2 - Mom could have identified with Angela's feelings by saying, "I know you are feeling especially tired today, and it's hard to get up and get going. But I really need your help with dinner." Angela might have responded with, "OK, but I'm right in the middle of this show. Can I just wait until it's over and then I'll do it?" There are lots of possibilities; help the kids think creatively about ways to keep the lines of communication open in these situations.)

When everyone is ready, reassemble the class and ask the groups to make their presentations.

Display the Unit Affirmation poster and ask the class to read the Affirmation aloud. Since this is the last class of the unit, review each of the phrases care-

Lesson 4

fully. Then ask the class to think of a final phrase to add today. Possibilities include, "by keeping the lines of communication open," or "by always using good communication skills." **Remember, learning to communicate well takes a lot of work! Using our skills will keep the lines of communication open with our friends and family. When we don't use our skills, barriers will go up that hurt ourselves and others in our lives. Let's look at a Bible story that shows just what can happen when we are not careful to keep the communication lines open.**

 # Searching the Scriptures (20 minutes)

Have students turn to II Samuel 13:38. By turning to the Scripture even when not reading directly from it, you establish the foundation that the student sheet isn't a fiction story, but based on facts gleaned from God's Word. **This story tells us about the problems that arose for King David and his son, Absalom, when the communication between them was broken. Let's see what happened.** Summarize the story as it is told in II Samuel 13:38–14:3, 12-24, 28, 32, 33. Distribute copies of the activity sheet, "The Complicated Case Of The Closed Communication" (page 84). This humorous take-off is written as a tongue twister. Let students take turns reading it aloud. Enjoy it and be ready for some laughs.

> **OPTIONAL:** If you have a longer class period, re-read the story with two of your best readers reading the parts of Holmes and Watson. The rest of the class can pantomime the actions of David, Absalom, the friend, and the old woman.

What were some of the problems caused by this lack of communication? (There was a separation physically, emotionally, and in their relationship.) **How did David feel about Absalom running away to his grandfather?** (He missed him and wanted to see him again.) **Were the problems solved when David allowed Absalom to return to Jerusalem? If not, why not?** (No. Even after they lived in the same town, the father and son never saw or talked to each other.)

Why do you think David's close friend, Joab, acted as go-between for David and Absalom? (Because he was a friend, knew they were both hurting and wanted to help them, felt their problem affected the nation as well as each other.) **Have you ever acted as a peacemaker for someone? What happened?** Encourage students who have had this experience to share it with the class. Be prepared to do so yourself if possible. For Joab, the position was not without cost. When he ignored Absalom's request that he be peacemaker a second time, Absalom burned Joab's fields in order to get his attention (II Samuel 14:30-32.)

How do you think Absalom felt about not seeing or hearing from his father? (Angry, disgusted, that his father didn't care about him.) **How did Absalom react to being treated as an outcast from the family?** (He rebelled, plotted against his father, tried to get even with David.) **Because David didn't clearly communicate the message of God's punishment for those who break His laws or the forgiveness that could be received upon confession of sin, Absalom slipped further into rebellion and disrespect. Allowing problems and misunderstandings to fester causes more pain and trouble than if they are dealt with right away. In this case the communication break eventually cost Absalom his life, and nearly cost David his kingdom.**

Father and son appear equally guilty. That David loved his wayward son is obvious in his anguished cry, "Oh my son. . . If only I had died instead of you" (II Samuel 18:33). And that Absalom, down in his heart, longed to see his father and get things straightened out is hinted at in II Samuel 14:32. But neither person seemed capable of laying aside personal feelings and reopening communication between them. This Bible story is a tragic example of what can happen when communication is closed.

How do you think these problems could have been solved? (By father and son talking things over.) **Is talking about misunderstandings enough?** Stress that such conversation needs to be carried out calmly. Losing tempers only leads to shouting, arguing, and fighting. The focus needs to be on the problem and trying to understand each other.

All the methods of good communication that have been taught in previous lessons in this unit apply to such a situation. Briefly review these together. Some of the methods to be remembered are: listen carefully, be sensitive to the feelings of others, disagree without getting angry, repeat anything that is unclear, be honest so others know what you are feeling or thinking, talk about the problem or action without attacking the other person's character. You may want to list these methods on the board for visual reinforcement.

☑ Living the Lesson (5-10 minutes)

What are some ways you can keep the lines of communication open? Divide the class into two or three small teams and have students brainstorm these techniques. Have each team write down all the ways they can come up with. After a short time, regroup and discuss their findings with the class. Some

methods that can be included are: write a note, call on the telephone, send a card, send a message via a friend, get someone to be a peacemaker or volunteer to be one yourself. Encourage kids to come up with a large quantity of ways, even those that on the surface may appear "far out." You can choose the most workable ways after discussing the quantity. Be sensitive to students who suggested rather different methods. Many great ideas have been by-passed originally as "crazy" or "ridiculous." Make your classroom a safe place where kids feel they can be open without fear of humiliation or criticism.

Have students look up Hebrews 1:2a and say it together. **How did Jesus keep the lines of communication open between a holy God and sinful people?** Explain that when He was alive, He showed and talked about God's forgiveness and how to get right with God. **When He died a sinless death, He tore down the wall of sin that stood between God and us. This made a permanent open channel for us to approach God. Now in Heaven, Jesus is always lovingly talking about us to His Father. If we ask God to forgive us and trust in Jesus' payment for our sin, we have access to God any time and any place.**

God was creative in the ways He chose to communicate with us in order to keep communication open. Explain that sometimes it is easier to express yourself by writing a note to someone than it is to speak. Everyone likes to receive a note because it makes him or her feel good. A note tells people you care enough to take the time and effort to personally communicate with them. You can get a loving message across quickly. Because a note can be re-read, it leaves a lasting impression. Notes don't shout or argue. Instead they encourage the writer to think clearly and calmly before communicating. They also encourage the recipient to respond in a similar manner.

Distribute writing materials. **Think about someone with whom you have a communication problem. Consider what you can say to that person to keep the lines open. Then write a note to him or her and share the friendship and love the Lord offers each of us.** Allow students a few minutes to write notes. Providing envelopes and stamps will encourage students to carry out this activity.

When we want to talk to God, we don't even have to write Him a note. Prayer allows us to communicate with our heavenly Father at all times and in all places. Close today's class by encouraging a time of individual silent prayer.

Am I Making Myself Perfectly Clear?

REWRITE _____

_____

_____

REWRITE _____

_____

_____

_____

The Complicated Case of the Closed Communications

What problems arise when communication between people is broken? Read through the story and look for clues as the famous detectives Sheer-luck Holmes and Dodger Watson solve this mystery.

Clever Sheer-luck Holmes and his capable crony, Dodger Watson, frowned as they studied the case. "This caper is confusing, Holmes. Do you think we can crack it?" Watson asked.

"Of course," Holmes replied. "Let's concentrate on the clues. This case has all the characteristics of common closed communications. First of all, this kid, Absalom, is only concerned with himself. A conceited character who breaks the law and becomes a criminal, he lacks courage to face the consequences. He cops-out and hurries off to his grandfather in a foreign country to cower in comfortable quarters. Meanwhile, back at the castle, his father, David, can't bring himself to correct his kid consistently. He loves his son, is crushed by his crime and cries a lot."

"He craves his son?" Watson cut in. "Then why doesn't he just contact him and call him home? He's the king so he can command the kid."

"Caution, Watson. To do so would make it appear that the king is collaborating with a crook. But the king's close friend, Joab, catches the cue. He contacts a clever woman who concocts a cloudy story that convicts the king of his inconsistency. The king consents to let the culprit come back into the country.

"Very cunning, Holmes. So the kid cleans up his act and connections are clear again."

"Not quite, Watson. The kid comes home and lives there for two years. But it's a cold coexistence. Wherever he goes, the king is conspicuous by his absence. Afraid of combat with his son, he cringes from correcting, convicting, or even criticizing him. Nor does he feel comfortable about condoning his crime. There is no coherent communication."

"Sounds like it's critical. Could there be a calamity coming?"

"Quite so, Watson. Like a deadly cancer, this chronic lack of correspondence creeps up to a crisis. The kid calls for the king's close friend again and asks him to carry a message to his father. He wants his father to cut his cruel conduct and either forgive or kill him."

"Wow! A drastic comment. He craves any kind of connection!"

"Correct! Well, the friend coaxes the king to crack his silence and contact his kid. To his credit, the king calls for his son to come see him."

"And when he does? All conflict is cancelled?" Watson questioned.

"Not quite. The king just never communicates God's laws and love to his son. Consequently, the kid thinks crime pays. He covertly campaigns to overthrow his father, corrupt the people and conquer the kingdom. He almost accomplishes his crooked scheme. Eventually however, he gets careless and causes his own destruction. What a climax!"

"Then both characters are to blame. What's the correct solution?"

"Use your cranium. The correct conduct is open communication. Calmly converse about problems. Confess feelings and consider the other person. Holmes, if I calculate right, this case is closed."

"Quite correct, Watson. Quite correct!"

Activity Sheet by Bev Gundersen © 1991 David C. Cook Publishing Co. Permission granted to reproduce for classroom use only.

Service Projects for Communicating With Others

In addition to the projects listed in these lessons your class or church can also serve in the following ways.

✔ 1. Use the designs for the T-shirts, lesson 2, on T-shirts or sweat shirts. Use fabric crayons as directed on the package and iron the design on or trace the designs with a textile-marking pen and paint them with fabric paints. The T-shirts could then be shared as you wish.

✔ 2. If role-plays in this unit are videotaped, make use of them for other classes or church intergenerational socials.

✔ 3. The skit "Quantum Leap Into Honesty," found in lesson 2, could be presented to another class or at a program to teach about communicating honestly with others.

✔ 4. Volunteer to write letters for the blind or visually impaired, nursing home and retirement home residents. Also ask if you can read to them and, if possible, locate reading materials of their choosing. In some communities, the Society for the Blind uses volunteers to read for tapes that the blind can rent or borrow.

✔ 5. Check to see if your area offers classes in sign language. Book stores and libraries have self-help books to teach signing. Learn to communicate with the hearing impaired in this special language.

✔ 6. Help newcomers to your community learn English. Become friends and make their adjustment to a new country less traumatic. You will also learn to appreciate other cultures and languages.

"Who Do You Say I Am?"

This question was first put to the disciples by Jesus almost 2,000 years ago (Matthew 16:13-16). Ever since that time, it has been the responsibility of all human beings to answer it for themselves. Today, the New Age movement has brought a renewed interest in spirituality to our country. Unfortunately, it has also introduced a theology in direct opposition to the teachings of the Bible. If your Juniors are to survive in the midst of the spread of this new religion, we must help them answer Jesus' soul searching question for themselves.

A story is told about a student who one day posed a question to his professor, a brilliant, well respected theologian. The question was this: "Of all the deep spiritual insights you have pondered over the years, which is the most profound?" The professor thought for a moment and then said, "Jesus loves me, this I know; for the Bible tells me so." In the weeks ahead, your kids will look to Scripture to ponder for themselves this simple and yet most profound eternal truth. As you review the Unit Verse and Unit Affirmation each week, they will be challenged to answer for themselves Jesus' question, "Who do YOU say that I am?" May you have the joy of hearing each of them affirm with Peter, "You are the Christ, the Son of the living God."

Who is Jesus Overview

Unit Verse: I am the way, the truth and the life. No one comes to the Father except through me. John 14:6
Unit Affirmation: I CAN KNOW JESUS PERSONALLY!

LESSON	TITLE	OBJECTIVE	SCRIPTURE BASE
Lesson #1	What a Friend We Have in Jesus	That your students will know that Jesus can help them because He experienced all the same feelings and problems they have.	Matthew 4:2; 16:13-17; 26:37, 38; Luke 4:28-30; 5:12, 13; John 2:12-16; 4:6; 6:66-70; 11:32-37; 12:1-3; 15:9; 21:15-18
Lesson #2	Will the Real Jesus Please Stand Up?	That your students will understand that Jesus was different from us because He is God's only Son.	Matthew 8:1-3; 14:22-33; Mark 1:23-27; 2:1-12; Luke 7:14-17; John 4:28, 29, 42; 6:5-13, 25; I Peter 2:21-25
Lesson #3	The Choice is Yours	That your students will be encouraged to not remain neutral about Jesus, but to accept Him as Lord and Savior.	John 10:24-38
Lesson #4	Just Gotta Tell	That your students will tell others what Jesus has done in their lives.	Acts 26:1-23

Partners

For the next few weeks your Junior-age child will be part of a group learning about Who Jesus is. *Partners* is a planned parent piece to keep you informed of what will be taught during this exciting series.

PREVIEW...

Who Is Jesus?

In Matthew 16:13-16, Jesus asked His disciples the question, "Who do you say I am?" Ever since that time, it has been the responsibility of all human beings to answer that question for themselves. Today, the New Age movement has brought a renewed interest in spirituality to our country. Unfortunately, it has also introduced a theology in direct opposition to the teachings of the Bible. If our kids are to survive in the midst of the spread of this new religion, we must help them answer Jesus' soul searching question for themselves.

A story is told about a student who one day posed a question to his professor, a brilliant, well respected theologian. The question was this: "Of all the deep spiritual insights you have pondered over the years, which is the most profound?" The professor thought for a moment and then said, "Jesus loves me, this I know; for the Bible tells me so." In the weeks ahead, your kids will look to Scripture to ponder for themselves this simple and yet most profound eternal truth. As they review the Unit Verse and Unit Affirmation each week, they will be challenged to answer for themselves Jesus' question, "Who do YOU say that I am?" It is our prayer that each of them will affirm with Peter, "You are the Christ, the Son of the living God."

Unit Verse:

I am the way, the truth and the life. No one comes to the Father except through me. John 14:6

Unit Affirmation:

I CAN KNOW JESUS PERSONALLY!

PRINCIPLES...

Who Is Jesus?

PRINCIPLE #1:

JESUS IS A FRIEND WHO HAS EXPERIENCED ALL THE SAME FEELINGS AND PROBLEMS WE HAVE. How many times have you heard your kids say, "You just don't understand!" All of us look for others who we believe will understand "where we're coming from." Most often that understanding comes from people who have felt and experienced the same things we have. Someone who has no idea what we're going through doesn't make for a very empathetic friend.

As your kids consider Jesus, they may feel a distance in that He is God and lived 2,000 years ago. Through reading the Gospels, however, we can see that Jesus has a very real understanding of our human experience. He felt tired, hungry, lonely, sad, happy, angry, and more. He told stories that illustrated His deep understanding of the human experience, and reassured us of God's love as a constant presence through all of life's experiences. Jesus' life on earth made it clear that God is not a distant God who cares little about His creation. Rather, He is a very personal, loving God who went to the greatest lengths possible to establish a relationship with us–He became one of us! No human friend can understand us better than that!

PRINCIPLE #2:

JESUS IS "THE CHRIST, THE SON OF THE LIVING GOD." A difficult point of theology for us to understand is that Jesus was both fully human and fully God. Although we want our kids to know Jesus as a friend who lived on earth and experienced all that we do, they must see Him as more. Jesus is also God, and we must give Him the worship and respect that being God deserves.

Jesus' divinity was clearly established by the miracles He performed and in the things He taught. This is summed up in Matthew 7:28, 29, "When Jesus had finished saying these things, the crowds were amazed at his teaching, because he taught as one who had authority, and not as their teachers of the law." Being God Himself, Jesus brings to us the very words of God and makes it possible for us to establish a relationship with Him. If He had been less than fully God, He could not have accomplished that for us.

PRINCIPLE #3:

JESUS MAKES A CLAIM ON OUR LIVES, TO WHICH EACH OF US MUST RESPOND PERSONALLY. Jesus puts the question, "Who do you say I am?" to each of us today. It is not possible to remain neutral about who He is. At some point, every human being must answer that question. As the Unit Verse affirms, Jesus is the source of eternal life, and no one comes to God except through a personal relationship with Him. Your Junior is old enough to consider Jesus' claim for him or herself and understand the commitment that is involved. This is an excellent age for kids to invite Jesus to be Lord and Savior of their lives!

PRINCIPLE #4:

KNOWING JESUS PERSONALLY IS GOOD NEWS THAT'S TOO GOOD TO KEEP TO OURSELVES! When we make discover-

ies that make our lives easier or happier, our first reaction is to find someone to tell. What greater news can there be to share with others than that we can know God personally, have His presence and power to help us through the circumstances of our lives, not to mention living with Him in heaven after we die? That's good news worth talking about!

PRACTICE...

Who Is Jesus?

1. RESPONDING TO THE CLAIMS OF JESUS.

If you have a personal relationship with Jesus, have you ever told your kids about it? They will be interested to hear about your spiritual journey and how you came to make a commitment to Christ.

If you do not have a relationship with Christ, perhaps now is a good time to seriously consider His claims on your life. If you have questions, make an appointment with your pastor or a Christian friend to talk about them. Deciding how you will respond to Christ is the most important decision you will ever make!

2. SHARING THE GOOD NEWS.

One of the best ways to teach your kids about sharing Christ with others is to reach out as a whole family to another family. Inviting them into your home, helping the kids to become friends, and responding to their needs will lead to natural opportunities to introduce them to Christ. It will also model for your children how to live out the spirit of Christ in our world.

3. SCRIPTURE SEARCH.

One way to discover who Jesus is, comes by studying the statements He makes about Himself. Look up the following verses and spend some time talking about them as a family. You could talk about a different one each day after dinner or at bed time. John 6:35; John 8:12; John 11:2; John 14:6 (Unit Verse); John 14:10-11; John 15:1, 5. Use these questions to guide your discussion: 1. What imagery does Jesus use to describe Himself? 2. What are the characteristics of the image? 3. How does the image help us understand who Jesus is? Example: Jesus is the way (John 14:6). The image of "the way" brings to mind a road or path to take us to a place we want to go. When we don't know the way, we get lost! Jesus keeps us from getting lost and leads us directly to the Father.

4. POSTER MAKING.

An added reinforcement would be to work together as a family to design a poster about each of the characteristics of Jesus you discover in the SCRIPTURE SEARCH.

Lesson 1

What a Friend We Have in Jesus

Aim: That your students will know that Jesus can help them because He experienced all the same feelings and problems they have.

Scripture: Matthew 4:2 (hunger); John 4:6 (weariness); John 6:66-70 (sadness); Matthew 26:37,38 (sorrow and trouble); Matthew 16:13-17 (happiness); John 15:9 (love); John 11:32-37 (grief); John 2:12-16 (anger); John 21:15-18 (forgiveness); Luke 5:12,13 (sympathy); John 12:1-3 (enjoyment); Luke 4:28-30 (rejection)

Unit Verse: I am the way, the truth and the life. No one comes to the Father except through me. John 14:6

Unit Affirmation: I CAN KNOW JESUS PERSONALLY!

Planning Ahead

1. Photocopy activity sheets (pages 95 and 96)-one for each student.
2. Prepare the Unit Affirmation poster by writing across the top of a large poster board: I CAN KNOW JESUS PERSONALLY! Under the title, write the numbers 1-4 down the left-hand side.
3. Chart out the hymn "O For A Thousand Tongues To Sing" according to the accent syllables of the lines shown in the illustration.

> O for a thousand tongues to sing
>
> My Great Redeemer's praise,
>
> The glories of my God and King,
>
> The triumphs of His grace.

1 Setting the Stage (5-10 minutes)

WHAT YOU'LL DO

- Write cards to Jesus telling Him why they are glad He is their friend

WHAT YOU'LL NEED

- Paper and markers, decorative trim (optional)

2 Introducing the Issue (20 minutes)

WHAT YOU'LL DO

- Brainstorm characteristics of people we pick as our friends
- Use an activity sheet to discover others in the class who are likely to be the most understanding friends
- Introduce the Unit Affirmation poster

WHAT YOU'LL NEED

- "Looking For Friends in All The Right Places" Activity Sheet (page 95)
- Unit Affirmation Poster

3 Searching the Scriptures (20 minutes)

WHAT YOU'LL DO

- Use an activity sheet and play a game to see that Jesus experienced the same feelings we have

WHAT YOU'LL NEED

- Bibles
- "A Friend For All Seasons" Activity Sheet (page 96)-one for every two students
- Spinners, dice or pennies; buttons, beans, or other playing pieces-one for each student
- Optional: paper, drawing supplies

4 Living the Lesson (5-10 minutes)

WHAT YOU'LL DO

- Optional: Draw comparison pictures to emphasize that Jesus can help us because He completely understands us and our problems
- Throughout this unit, students will write original verses for the hymn, "O For A Thousand Tongues To Sing." Write a verse about the humanity of Jesus.

WHAT YOU'LL NEED

- Copies of hymn—"O For A Thousand Tongues To Sing"
- Optional: Rhyming dictionary, thesaurus

89

 *Lesson 1*

 # Setting the Stage (5-10 minutes)

Before class write the following on the board: "WHAT A FRIEND WE HAVE IN JESUS!" Set up the tables with paper, markers, glue and a few trims such as yarn, lace doilies, glitter, ribbon, etc. As your students arrive, ask them to read the message on the board. **Use the supplies on your table to write a letter or card to Jesus telling Him why you are glad He is your friend.** As they work, circulate among them, encouraging them to write specific reasons why they are glad Jesus is their friend. Be prepared for this to be difficult! Most of your kids will write general statements like, "You're the best!", or "Thanks for being my friend." Tell them to say *why* He's the best, or why they are glad He's their friend.

Ask for volunteers to read their cards to the rest of the class. **How many of you had trouble thinking of specific reasons why you are glad Jesus is your friend?** Give the kids an opportunity to respond. **Maybe some of you even had trouble thinking of Jesus as a friend at all! Today we are beginning a new unit about who Jesus is. In the next few weeks, we will talk about how each of us can not only know about who He is, but actually know Him personally as a friend.**

 # Introducing the Issue (20 minutes)

To understand how Jesus can be our friend, we have to first of all think about what it means to be friends with someone. What are the characteristics of people we would like to be our friends? As kids share their responses, write them on the board. Possible answers include: Like the same things we do, live in the same neighborhood or go to the same school, love us, listen to us, share our secrets, etc. Encourage the kids to think creatively and come up with as many characteristics as they can.

Distribute copies of the activity sheet, "Looking For Friends In All the Right Places," (page 95). **Let's try an experiment. Let's see how much potential we have for friendships right here in our class.** Give the kids time to write out their answers to complete the statements on the sheet, leaving the line for OTHERS blank. Then give the following instructions, allowing time for them to complete each one before going on to the next one.

1. Find someone in our class who answered ONE question the same or almost the same as you did. Write that person's name on the OTHERS line under the question that is the same.

2. Find someone who answered THREE questions the same or almost the same as you. Write that person's name on the line under each of the questions that are the same.

3. Find someone who answered FIVE questions the same or almost the same as you. Write that person's name on the line below those questions.

4. Find as many other classmates as you can that answered EIGHT or more of the questions the same as you did. Write their names on the lines under each question.

Now look at your sheets. Who do you think are the other kids in class who might be good friends for you? (The ones who answered many of the questions the same.) **Why do you think we pick people as friends who have many of the same things in common with us?** (Because they will want to do the things we want to do, they will go the places we go, be able to talk to us about things we want to talk about, etc.) **The bottom line is, we want to be friends with people who will understand us. Understanding comes from experiencing the same things or being interested in the same things. For example, if you wanted to be on a soccer (or Little League, or whatever sport you kids are into) team, who from our class might you ask to join with you?** (Someone who also has an interest in that sport.) **Supposing you asked me to join, and I hate playing soccer! I might say something like, "Are you kidding? Why would I want to do something like run around a field chasing a dumb ball, getting all hot and sweaty? I can't understand why anyone would want to do that!"**

Now suppose your parents got a divorce. Who might you seek out in that case? (Someone else whose parents had gotten a divorce.) **Why?** (Because that person is much more likely to understand how you are feeling and be able to help you get through the rough times.)

What if you listed the place you most want to visit as the North Pole. Who would you ask to go with you? (Someone who likes snow and cold and also wants to visit the North Pole.) **Anyone who hates the cold and snow will not be able to share your dream of going to the North Pole!**

Display the Unit Affirmation poster and have the class read the Affirmation aloud together. **Earlier today we talked about Jesus being our friend. How can Jesus be our friend when He is God and lives in heaven, and we are human and live on earth?** Allow for responses. **In a few minutes, we are going to discover from the Bible that Jesus is a friend who understands us completely, because when He was here on earth, He experienced so many of the same things and feelings we do.** Write the phrase, "Because He understands me completely," on the first line of the poster. **It is really exciting to find out how much Jesus has in common with us. Let's play a game to help us do that.**

✓ Searching the Scriptures (20 minutes)

We often sing "What A Friend We Have In Jesus." We know that Jesus is God's Son. Do you think He can really know how you feel or where you are coming from? Answers will vary but most kids feel that because Jesus never sinned, He couldn't possibly understand them. Also, He lived in "olden times" and didn't have to face the modern problems they do. Divide your class into pairs. Give a copy of the activity sheet "A Friend For All Seasons," (page 96) to each pair. Playing this game will help them understand that He was fully human and therefore had all the feelings and problems they have.

Use a spinner, die, or penny to decide how far each player moves at one time. If you use a penny, heads means two spaces and tails means one space. Use odd buttons or dried beans as playing pieces. Read the directions aloud.

1. The player with the earliest birth date starts.

2. If you land on a space with directions, you must follow them.

3. See if you can identify the events in Jesus' life that correspond with it without looking up the reference. If not, look up the verses and read them aloud. What is the feeling that Jesus might have felt in each situation?

4. The first player to reach "Finish" wins.

Allow kids to play for 5-10 minutes. Answers to Jesus' feelings are: hunger, enjoyment, anger, love, weariness, sorrow and trouble, sympathy, rejection, happiness, depression, forgiveness, grief. Stop play. Have students name the feelings and compare them with those people have today. If some of the feelings were not mentioned, have students look up their references and read them aloud. **What did playing this game show you about Jesus?** (He had the same feelings we do.)

> **OPTIONAL:** Hand out drawing materials and have students divide their papers in half. Have them choose a feeling they can relate to from among those you discussed and write it at the top of their paper. Think of a time when Jesus felt like that and draw a picture of it on the left side of your paper and save the right side until later. As they do this guide the conversation to focus on Jesus' feelings and reactions to situations. How did Jesus feel about this situation? How did He react to it? How did He treat others around Him when this happened? Did it change His relationship with God, His Father? Did it change His relationship with others? If so, how?

Were the events and feelings Jesus had similar to any you have had? Help your kids understand that Jesus was very much a human being with all the same feelings they experience. **Why do you think God's Son went**

through these times of stress and sadness? (So Jesus can sympathize with us, know how to help us.) **Why do you think God put these experiences in the Bible for us to read?** (To help us realize that Jesus was also human and understands us.) Point out that Jesus is the one and only God-Man. Because of that He alone can help us.

How does knowing Jesus weathered the same kinds of problems you have make you feel? (Glad, relieved, more apt to depend on Him when I need help.) **Nothing is more frustrating to us than to try to explain how we feel about a situation to someone and discover s/he just can't sympathize with us or understand why we feel the way we do about it.**

If you have a longer class period, students can do a more in-depth study of the humanity and understanding of Jesus. Further passages to consider are: Hebrews 2:10-18; 4:14-18; and 5:7-9.

 # Living the Lesson (5-10 minutes)

We can be thankful to God that Jesus understands how we feel.

> **Optional:** Have students return to the drawings they made earlier. On the right side of your paper show how Jesus might help you handle that same feeling today. As they do this guide the conversation to focus on the help of Jesus. What difference could having Jesus as your friend make in this situation? What added resources can He give you to help you deal with tough problems? Can He change your attitude about things? If so, how?
>
> Encourage students to share their drawings with the class, but be sensitive to any who appear embarrassed to do so. Remember that you want to make your class a safe, comfortable place where your students can feel secure to deal with the things that trouble them. Essentially the most personal problems are between the kids and God.

Have students turn to John 14:6 and read it together. **Sometimes it feels as though nobody really understand us. We wonder why we feel the way we do or how to face the problems we have.** Help your students see that Jesus understands them. Jesus is one friend we can always turn to for help and sympathy. Because He was human He is sensitive to our needs. Because He is God, He can help us.

Explain that because Jesus is both God and human, He can show people the way to find God. He is the go-between, the intermediary, the negotiator for both the holy, sinless God, and sinful humans. Because He alone knows both sides, Jesus is the one and only person who can fix our broken link with God.

By uniting our lives with Jesus, our broken relationship with our heavenly Father is restored and our lives have a new direction and purpose.

Students remember something set to music much better than merely memorizing it. Having a part in the creation of their own "class hymn" about Jesus will reinforce the lessons in this unit. Explain that throughout this unit the class will write original verses for the hymn, "O For A Thousand Tongues To Sing." **Today we are going to write about how Jesus can help us because He experienced the same feelings and problems we have.** Distribute copies of the song.

Display the hymn chart. **This chart shows us where the accents are in the song. The first and third lines each have four accents. The second and fourth each have three. When we write, we want to match our word accents with the beats that are shown.** Students can make suggestions and you can write the "finished" verse on the board or a large sheet of paper. Your song does not have to rhyme. You can rhyme only part or none of it. As long as you carry out the same accent rhythm you will be able to sing it easily. An example is:

Jesus, our friend and Savior kind,
Can help us with our needs.
For He has felt our joys and pains,
And He understands and cares.

Sing your class hymn together. Have students pray silently asking Jesus to help them with one specific problem or need. Close by thanking Him for willing to become a man who can fully understand and help us.

Looking For Friends in All the Right Places

1. My school is _____

Others: _____

2. My teacher is _____

Others: _____

3. My favorite food is _____

Others: _____

4. My hobbies are _____

Others: _____

5. Lessons I take are _____

Others: _____

6. Teams I am on are _____

Others: _____

7. My parents are divorced: Yes   No

Others: _____

8. My family moved sometime within the last year: Yes No

Others: _____

9. The place in the world I would most like to visit is _____

Others: _____

10. My worst subject in school is _____

Others: _____

11. My best subject in school is _____

Others: _____

12. The thing I am most afraid of is _____

Others: _____

A Friend For All Seasons

Parents getting Divorced. Lose turn. (Matthew 26:37, 38)

Walked 10 miles for World Relief. Ahead 1. (John 4:6)

Invited AIDS classmate home for sleepover. Extra turn (Luke 5:12, 13)

Have to move and leave friends. Back 1. (John 6:66-70)

I'M SORRY...

Accept friend's apology and remain friends. Ahead 1. (John 21:15-18)

THAT'S OKAY!

MY PAL!

Blew winning play. Team shuns you. Back 2. (Luke 4:28-30)

Friend congratulates you for winning award. Ahead 2. (Matthew 16:13-17)

RIP

Friend killed in accident. Lose turn. (John 11:32-37)

You and best friend do everything together. Ahead 2 (John 15:9)

FUN!

Bully beats up your little brother. Back 1. (John 2:12-16)

POW!

Finish **WINNER**

Start

LUNCH

Team practice, missed lunch. Back to Start. (Matthew 4:2)

GO TEAM

Friend gives you his pro-game ticket. Ahead 1. John 12:1-3

Lesson 2 ✔

Will the Real Jesus Please Stand Up?

Aim: That your students will understand that Jesus was different from us because He is God's only Son.

Scripture: Matthew 8:1-3 (healed people/Lord); Matthew 14:22-33 (controlled nature/Son of God); John 4:28,29,42 (knew everything people did/Christ/Savior); Luke 7:14-17 (raised the dead to life/prophet/God); Mark 2:1-12 (forgave sins/Son of Man/God); John 6:5-13,25 (fed great crowds of people/Rabbi/Teacher); Mark 1:23-27 (cast out evil spirits/Holy One of God); I Peter 2:21-25 (never sinned, died for our sins, lives again/Shepherd)

Unit Verse: I am the way, the truth and the life. No one comes to the Father except through me. John 14:6

Unit Affirmation: I CAN KNOW JESUS PERSONALLY!

✔ Planning Ahead

1. Copy last week's student written verse for the class hymn on a large sheet of poster board. Leave room for the three remaining verses of this unit.
2. Prepare a "J" object lesson for the Bible study as described in SEARCHING THE SCRIPTURES.
3. Photocopy activity sheets (pages 103 and 104)-one for each student.

1 | Setting the stage (5-10 minutes)

WHAT YOU'LL DO

- Participate in an exercise of describing others to begin thinking about how we know what people are like

WHAT YOU'LL NEED

- Paper and pencils

2 | Introducing the Issue (20 minutes)

WHAT YOU'LL DO

- Use an activity sheet to experience finding out about others through interviews, eyewitness accounts and giving testimonies.
- Add a phrase to the Unit Affirmation poster

WHAT YOU'LL NEED

- "NEWS FLASH!" Activity Sheet (page 103)
- Unit Affirmation poster

3 | Searching the Scriptures (20 minutes)

WHAT YOU'LL DO

- Complete a crossword puzzle using the reports of eyewitnesses as clues to see Jesus in action
- View an object lesson to understand how faith in Jesus and His claims grew as a result of His actions

WHAT YOU'LL NEED

- Bibles
- "The Name Game" Activity Sheet (page 104)
- "J" object lesson
- Optional: choir robe, gavel, hammer or large spoon

4 | Living the Lesson (5-10 minutes)

WHAT TO DO

- Contrast what Jesus did with what ordinary people can do and draw some personal conclusions from this comparison
- Write a hymn verse about Jesus, the divine Son of God.

WHAT YOU'LL NEED

- Chalkboard and chalk or a marker and large sheet of paper
- Copies of "O For A Thousand Tongues To Sing," syllable accent chart from "Who Is Jesus?" Lesson One, marker
- Optional: Rhyming dictionary, thesaurus

Setting the Stage (5-10 minutes)

As your students arrive today, instruct them to begin thinking about a relative they can describe to the class. This can be mom, dad, grandparent, aunt, uncle, etc. Tell them that they will be able to say anything they want to help the class get to know this relative, but they must keep the physical description to one sentence, and then go on to other characteristics. Give them time to write down the things they would like to say. As they work, circulate among them, helping them think of things to include. The possibilities include actions, character qualities, accomplishments, interests, anecdotes that illustrate their personalities, etc. After a few minutes, give each one a chance to describe their relative to the class. (NOTE: If your class is large, divide into two or three groups for this sharing time.)

How many of you had a hard time thinking of things to say? Most of them probably will have a difficult time. They may not be used to describing people in terms other than physical descriptions. **What are the things that help us know what a person is really like?** (Actions, character qualities, accomplishments, interests, etc.) **Today we are going to continue our study of Jesus by looking at some of His actions, character qualities and accomplishments as a way to get to know Him better.**

Introducing the Issue (20 minutes)

Before we can talk about getting to know more about Jesus, we must spend some time talking about how we get to know others. Getting to know others is one of the most fun and interesting parts of life. In fact, we spend a great deal of time collecting information about other people. Who are the people we are gathering information about? (Family, friends, neighbors, pastors at church, teachers, classmates, people in the news, TV stars, etc.) **How do we get to know about these people?** (Talking to them, watching what they do and say, reading about them, talking to other people who know them, etc.) The point to emphasize here is that there are many ways to get to know another person. Personal contact is only one. We also learn by hearing what others say about them and by careful observation of their actions. That is the heart of how we come to know Jesus. In Scripture we learn what Jesus is like from reading eyewitness accounts of His words and actions. We also know what Jesus is like by hearing other Christians talk about what it means to them to be a Christian. Your students need to see these as valid ways of collecting information about others so they will be able to trust these same methods to know Jesus personally.

Distribute copies of the activity sheet, "NEWS FLASH!", (page 103). **Let's see if we can understand more about these methods of getting to know others by becoming reporters for a few minutes.** Divide the class into pairs and ask them to fill out questions one through four of the activity sheet by interviewing their partners. When they are finished, give a few more minutes for them to interact with other classmates to gather information for question five. When they have all this information, ask them to spend a few minutes more writing up a news release on the person they interviewed. This need only be a few sentences, but should capture the essence of the data they collected.

When these are complete, collect all the sheets and mix them up. Then read the first one to the class without telling them who the NEWS FLASH is about. Now ask the class to guess who the person is, based on the information they heard. When they figure out who it is, go on to the next one. Repeat the process until all have been read. **What new things did you learn about your classmates today?** Allow for responses. Kids can pick out specific details of things they didn't know about each other. **Is there anyone you feel you might like to get to know better, based on something you learned today?** Perhaps someone in your class will discover a common interest or experience with another classmate that neither of them realized they shared. They might like to talk more about it at another time. **What methods did we use to discover this new information and new potential friends?** (Personal contact - interviews; eyewitness accounts - talking to other classmates; reading/ hearing reports about others - listening to the NEWS FLASHES being read to them.)

We have just practiced learning to know others by finding out new information about them. We have seen that it is possible to get to know another person by many different means. Now we want to spend some time using those same methods to see what we can discover about who Jesus is. What methods can we use to do that? (Read about Him in the Bible, ask others who know Him to tell us about Him.) **In a minute, we will see what we can learn by looking at the Bible. But first, let me tell you what Jesus means to me.** Illustrate how we can know what Jesus is like through the testimony of other Christians by sharing what it means to you to know Jesus personally.

Display the Unit Affirmation poster and ask the class to read the Affirmation aloud together. **Last week we discovered that we can know Jesus as a friend who understands everything we go through. What can we write**

on the second line today that will help us know Jesus personally? A possibility might be, "by listening to what others say about Him and by reading about Him in the Bible." **Now let's see if we can get to know Jesus better by seeing what others have said and written about Him in the Bible.**

 # Searching the Scriptures (20 minutes)

Before class, make a "J" object lesson by folding a piece of 8 1/2" x 11" piece of paper in half to form a sheet 8 1/2" x 5 1/2". Continue to fold the paper three more times, mak-ing it 5 1/2" x 4 1/4", 4 1/4" x 2 3/4", and finally 2 3/4" x 2 1/8". Unfold the paper and using a yellow crayon, make a series of different sized letter J's as shown. Make the final "J" on the opposite side of the paper. Fold the paper, with the largest letter inside.

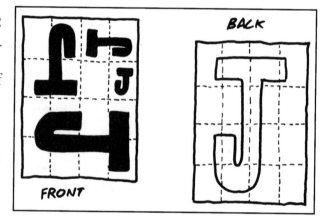

Let's see what can we discover about Jesus. We'll look at some of the things He did and find out what people of His day thought about Him. Distribute copies of the activity sheet "The Name Game", (page 104). Ask someone to read the directions. Students will work on this puzzle individually. Be aware of any kids who are having difficulty or are not familiar enough with the Bible to locate references. (Answers. Down: Man, shepherd, prophet, Lord, Son. Across: teacher, Holy, Savior.)

Allow time to work on this activity and then discuss it together. **What were some of the names people assigned to Jesus?** (Teacher, prophet, shepherd, Holy One of God, Christ, Savior, Son of God, etc.) **These comments about Him show us that they realized Jesus was more than a carpenter's son.**

What caused them to think this? (He could do things people couldn't do, He did things only God can do.) **What were some of these things?** (Control nature, feed thousands of people with only a little food, know everything about people, die and live again.)

As Jesus did miracle after miracle, people were astonished and their faith in Him grew. Display the object lesson you prepared before class by holding it up, folded, in the palm of your left hand. Can anyone tell me what I am holding? Students will have difficulty doing this because it is so small. Ask someone to step forward and identify the tiny "J."

Explain the object lesson similar to this: **This is the way most people thought of Jesus when He began His public ministry. They thought of Him as merely the carpenter from the little country village of Nazareth. Then He performed His first miracle at a wedding in Cana**. Unfold the paper one fold, displaying the next size "J." **Then came the time He quieted the storm on the Sea of Galilee. His followers were amazed and thought of Him as the Son of God.** Unfold paper to reveal the next size letter.

As time went on and the people saw other miracles, their opinion of Jesus grew and they expressed this in the names they gave Him. Keep unfolding the paper to reveal larger letters. As you do so, mention some of the other miracles and names from the puzzle. Hold up the largest "J." Now every-one here can see the letter. **Jesus wants people everywhere to know that He is more than a man.**

Explain that Jesus wants us to believe that He is exactly who He said He was and all the claims about Him are true. In a visible, tangible way, Jesus showed people what God was like. Because He is more than a mere man, we need to give Him the respect and honor we give God.

Today we're going to have a trial to let you decide if Jesus is really God's Son. You will be jurors at our court trial. Divide your class into pairs. Depending on the size of your class, assign each pair one or more of the Bible passages given in the crossword puzzle. Each pair of jurors is to compare the deeds of Jesus described in its verses with work done by ordinary people. Be ready to share your conclusions with the group.

Every judge has the right to instruct the jury as to what basis it should use to judge the defendant. As "judge" in this trial you can also instruct the members of your jury. **As you study the evidence of these witnesses, remember that if ordinary people can perform the same actions, then Jesus is guilty of fraud. He is only a man. If His actions are supernatural, then He must be who He says He is. He is God's Son.**

Have the class regroup after a few minutes. Depending upon the age and maturity of your students, you may want to encourage kids to think harder about the contrast between Jesus and ordinary people by assuming the role of an "unbelieving questioner." For example, modern medicine has made possible many seemingly miraculous happenings. A machine that can recirculate the blood during a heart transplant operation is marvelous enough to cause great awe. Generate deeper reflection on the part of students by asking how this differs from the healings Jesus did. Your purpose here is to stimulate your Juniors to think for themselves and not merely repeat surface answers. This gives them practical preparation within the safe confines of the classroom which will enable them to face unbelieving criticism in the secular world.

Lesson 2

As each pair shares its conclusions, make a comparison chart on the board or poster board. Divide the chart into two columns with the headings "People" and "God." Write the event on the left side and then indicate whether people or God could do what is described in each set of Bible verses.

After all the evidence has been recorded, conclude your "trial." **Ladies and gentlemen of the jury, what final verdict do you reach? How do you find the defendant, Jesus? Is He or is He not the Son of God?**

> **OPTIONAL:** If your class enjoys drama, add to the realism of this activity by carrying out the trappings of a courtroom. You, as judge, can wear a choir robe and use a gavel, hammer, or large spoon to pound as you announce the verdict and adjourn the "court." A student could be the court reporter and write the findings on the board.

Living the Lesson (5-10 minutes)

Have students look up John 14:6 and repeat it together. Point out that a professional singer has a certain style that is distinctly his or her own. By merely listening to a song people are able to identify the singer. **What could people know by looking at the miracles Jesus performed?** (The power of God at work, the mark of God was on each deed.) **Jesus was indeed the Son of God. He is the same as God.**

Jesus said that He was the Truth. What do you think this meant to the people of His day? Let students think about this before offering any suggestions. Before Jesus came, the Jews were the people who really knew what the real God was like. The people who were not Jews knew little or nothing about God. When Jesus came, He provided both Jews and non-Jews with the truth about God. Now non-Jews were equal with Jews and both groups could be saved from sin.

Have students work together to write another verse for the class hymn about Jesus as God's Son–equal with His heavenly Father. Remind them to observe the accents of the song and to match words with them. An example for today might be:

Jesus, the Christ, did miracles
That showed His mighty power.
They proved He was the Way, the Truth,
For He is God's own, dear Son.

Sing both last week's and today's verses of your class hymn together. Encourage your students to share one reason they are glad that Jesus is God's Son.

News Flash! ✓

We have just discovered that this class is hiding some very important and prestigious kids! You are assigned to interview one of them, and then write a NEWS FLASH to let everyone else in the class know what a terrific person this is!

Reporter _____

Interviewee (your partner)_____

✏ Interview Questions:

1. Find out something about this person that no one in the class already knows.

_____

2. What is this person's best character quality (kind, funny, good listener,etc.)?

_____

3. What special hobbies, interests, awards or achievements?

_____

4. What plans for the future?

_____

5. Eyewitness account: Find someone else in the class who knows this person and can verify most of the above info, and add one new piece of information:

_____

✏ NEWS FLASH!

In this space, use all of the above information to write a news release describing your person to the rest of the class.

_____

_____

_____

_____

_____

_____

_____

_____

_____

The Name Game

Read the clues and complete the puzzle with some of the names that Jesus was called. If you need help, use the Bible references to look up the verses.

Down

1. Forgave sins, "Son of_____"—Mark 2:1-12
2. Never sinned, died for our sins, lives again—I Peter 2:21-25
3. Raised the dead to life—Luke 7:14-17
6. Healed people—Matthew 8:1-3
7. Controlled nature, "_____ of God"—Matthew 14:22-33

Across

4. Fed great crowds of people, "Rabbi" means _____—John 6:5-13, 25
5. Cast out evil spirits "_____ One of God"—Mark 1:23-27
7. Knew everything people did, "Christ" is the _____ of the world—John 4:28,29,42

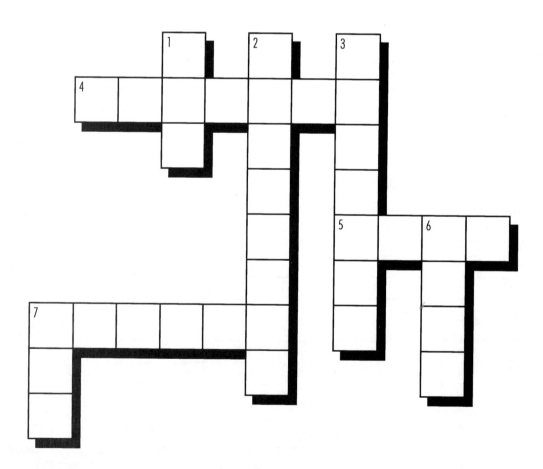

The Choice is Yours

Aim: That your students will be encouraged to not remain neutral about Jesus, but to accept Him as Lord and Savior.
Scripture: John 10:24-38
Unit Verse: I am the way, the truth and the life. No one comes to the Father except through me. John 14:6
Unit Affirmation: I CAN KNOW JESUS PERSONALLY!

 Planning Ahead

1. Copy the student written verse from last week onto the poster board of the class hymn.
2. Photocopy activity sheets (pages 111 and 112)-one for each student.

1 Setting the Stage (5-10 minutes)
WHAT YOU'LL DO
- Play "Follow the Leader"

WHAT YOU'LL NEED
- No supplies needed

2 Introducing the Issue (20 minutes)
WHAT YOU'LL DO
- Brainstorm the effects leaders have on us that make us want to follow them
- Use an activity sheet to write appeals for followers
- Add a phrase to the Unit Affirmation poster

WHAT YOU'LL NEED
- "Follow the Leader" Activity Sheet (page 111)
- Unit Affirmation poster

3 Searching the Scriptures (20 minutes)
WHAT YOU'LL DO
- Use an activity sheet and read a radio news broadcast to emphasize the effect and claim Jesus made on the lives of those around Him

WHAT YOU'LL NEED
- Bibles
- "Jerusalem Investigative Report" Activity Sheet (page 112)

4 Living the Lesson (5-10 minutes)
WHAT YOU'LL DO
- Use a "Feetograph" to respond to an opportunity to receive Jesus as Savior and Lord
- Write a verse for the class hymn focusing on the salvation that Jesus provides for those who trust in Him and choose to follow Him

WHAT YOU'LL NEED
- Large sheets of paper–one for each student
- Copies of "O For A Thousand Tongues To Sing," syllable accent chart from "Who Is Jesus?" Lesson One, poster board copy of class hymn
- Optional: Rhyming dictionary, thesaurus

...age (5-10 minutes)

...day, involve them in a game of Follow the Leader.
... lead them in a series of movements which they
... might choose a succession of physical movements,
such as touching your toes, running in place, hopping on one foot, hugging
your neighbor, etc. After a few minutes, stop and invite a volunteer to be the
leader. Be sure to choose someone who can think quickly and will keep the
game moving. As time allows, invite others to be the leader.

OPTIONAL: If you have a longer class session, you may want to include this
variation of Follow the Leader. Ask the class to select partners and designate
one person to be the leader. To play, the partners stand facing each other and
the leader begins a series of movements, which the partner must follow exactly. This could be making faces, arm movements or simple body movements
that can be done while standing in one place. After a few minutes, switch roles
and let the partner become the leader.

**Who would you say in our class are talented "Follow the Leader"
leaders?** Let kids respond. **From our game, would you conclude that some
leaders are easier to follow than others?** That will no doubt be their experience. **Does the fact that someone wants to be a leader mean they will be
a good leader?** (Not necessarily; desire and skill are not automatically connected) **Today we are going to talk about what it means to follow many
kinds of leaders, and how we can make choices about which leaders are
good for us to follow. We will also talk about how Jesus is a leader who
demands we choose whether or not we will be His followers.**

  # Introducing the Issue (20 minutes)

**During your lifetime, you will be faced with many decisions about
whether or not you will follow someone's leadership. Who are some of
the people in your lives that demand your attention and want you to
follow them?** (Political candidates in government, school, and other organiza-
tions; teachers; coaches; religious leaders; entertainment stars; merchants who
ask us to follow by buying their products; etc.) **How do they try to get us to
follow them?** (Making speeches, promising they will do things for us, meeting
our needs in some way, advertising, etc.) **Sometimes we say that a certain**

leader "has a following." What do you think that means? (A following is a group of people who have made a decision to follow that leader.) **What are some reasons why you might choose to follow someone?** (You believe their promises and that they will do something for you, you want something they have to offer, you like them, etc.)

Distribute copies of the activity sheet, "Follow the Leader", (page 111). Divide the class into four groups and assign each group one of the scenarios. Give them a few minutes to follow the directions and write their statements. As they work, circulate among the groups to give suggestions and direction to groups that may need a little extra help. When they are finished, gather the class together again. **Each of you may now present your statements. You will have to convince us that we should follow your leadership, and when you are finished we will decide if we want to be your followers or not.** Now let each group make their presentation. Talk about each one. **What promises were made? Do you believe them? Why or why not? What do you have to do as a follower? Why might you want to follow this person? Why wouldn't you want to follow this person? How will you respond?** Guide your kids to see that there are essentially three responses we can have to those who try to get us to follow their leadership. They are:

1. Become a loyal follower. In this case, you choose to believe the promises and make a commitment to do whatever the leader asks you to do.

2. Reject the leader. In this case, you do not believe the promises being made, and do not want to do what the leader asks of you.

3. Be a skeptic. We may not know whether following the leader is the right thing or not, and decide not to do anything about the leader's claims.

It is important for each of us to learn how to evaluate the claims of those around us who want to be our leaders. Whether we are deciding to buy a certain product, or vote for a certain candidate, we must make careful decisions. The same is true about Jesus. He is a leader who makes a claim on our lives. In a few minutes, we are going to look at the Bible to see how Jesus confronted the people in His day to make a decision about Him. Then we will see that He asks us to make a decision about whether or not each of us will follow Him. Each of us has the same three choices as we've just talked about. We can accept Him as our leader, reject Him, or be skeptical.

Display the Unit Affirmation poster and review it. Then write, "by accepting His claims of leadership over my life," on the third line. **Of course, not everyone chooses to accept Jesus' leadership. Let's see what else we can learn from seeing how people in Jesus' day responded to His claims.**

✓ Searching the Scriptures (20 minutes)

Have students turn to John 10:24-38 and take turns reading it. **Jesus had a powerful effect on people around Him, didn't He? Let's take a look at this Bible-times news broadcast done by an investigative team to help us find out why they reacted so strongly.** Distribute copies of the activity sheet "Jerusalem Investigative Report", (page 112). Choose four students to read the parts. To add to the realism of this activity use a disconnected microphone, or substitute large spoons and have your correspondents give their reports from different areas of the classroom.

What does "Christ" mean? (The person chosen by God to save people from their sins.) **"Christ" or Messiah was a term used for Jesus who came to be a mediator or peacemaker.** Explain that when two people get into a conflict they need a mediator to bring peace between them. When Adam and Eve sinned against God, they needed a mediator to bring peace between them and God. Have someone look up I Timothy 2:5, 6a and read it aloud. **Who is the mediator between God and sinful people?** (Jesus.)

How did the people in this Bible story in John react to Jesus? (Some got mad at Him, tried to kill Him.) **Why did people want to kill Jesus?** (Because He indicated that He was God.) **What did Jesus say about the miracles He had done?** (They were done by the power of God, they had the power to convince people He was God.)

Why do you think God helped Jesus to get away safely in this circumstance but allowed Him to die on the cross? Explain that if Jesus had died here He could not have died in the way the prophets had said the Christ would die. More importantly Jesus needed to give up His life of His own choice to pay for the sins of all people. Only in that way could He become the exclusive way to God.

If Jesus is the Christ and wanted everyone to come to God through Him, why do you think He made it so hard for people to follow Him? Briefly point out the differences between modern political campaigns with the way Jesus talked with people. Candidates try to get people to vote for them by acting friendly and making various promises they can't keep. They frequently don't tell the truth. Jesus is the Truth as well as the Way. He made people understand that following Him meant obeying God and returning their lives to His control. He promised them eternal life and forgiveness of their sins. Because He is God's Son, He has the power to keep those promises.

Have someone look up John 1:3, 4 and read it aloud. **Who is this passage talking about?** (Jesus.) **Who made you?** (Jesus.) To help students understand the claim that their Creator, Jesus, has on them read this story:

Scott loved to make and fly model airplanes. It took him a long time to put his favorite one together but when he was done, the plane was perfect in every detail. He hurried to the park to fly it. The plane taxied across the grass and soared into the sky. It banked and turned, obeying Scott's commands. Suddenly something went wrong. The plane refused to respond. It disappeared over the trees.

Later Scott sadly watched other kids flying planes. He noticed a boy tinkering with a plane like his. "Can I see your plane?" Scott asked. "Sure," the boy answered. "I found it stuck in a bush." Scott looked under the wings. There were his initials. "That plane is mine," Scott said. "Finders, keepers! If you want it back you'll have to buy it," the boy declared. "But, I made it! See my initials here?" Scott pointed them out.

The boy refused to give in. Scott had to use his savings money to buy the plane. "Now you're doubly mine, little plane," he said. "I made you and I bought you."

How is this story like what Jesus did? (He made us and after we disobeyed, He died to buy us back.) Explain that the process of buying us back is called "redemption." Because Jesus redeemed us He has a legitimate claim on the life of every person. But not everyone admits that claim.

Have students turn to John 14:6 and say it aloud. **How is Jesus the Way to God?** (He knows God because He is God's Son, died to become the Savior of the world.) Help the kids to understand that before Jesus came the priests and rabbis had a partial understanding of God's Word. When the rabbis taught in the synagogues, they repeated the explanations their ancestors had repeated for centuries. Jesus gave the true, complete disclosure or picture of what God was like.

Jesus paid for our sin by dying in our place. Because He is God and Man He is the only way to find God. By His sinless life, willing death, and resurrection to everlasting life Jesus made it possible for people to be saved from death, punishment for sin, and eternal separation from God.

Make sure your students understand what is involved in salvation. **If Jesus has already paid the price for our sin, what is our part in salvation?** (We need to agree with God that we have done wrong things and followed our own desires. We admit that we are sinners.)

What happens when we receive Jesus? When we ask God to forgive our sin, Jesus becomes our Savior. When we turn the control of our life over to Him, decide to obey His rules, and follow His guidance, Jesus becomes our Lord.

✓ Living the Lesson (5-10 minutes)

Distribute large sheets of paper. Have the Juniors stand on the paper and draw around their feet. **You have just made a Feetograph! If you have decided to become a follower of Jesus and are willing to receive Him as your Savior and Lord, sign your feetograph. Also write today's date on it.** Explain that kids can look back on this day as their spiritual birthday. Some may already have made this decision and can write that date if they prefer. In the future if they are troubled with doubts about whether they are part of God's family, they can remember this date and know that it was the day they chose to receive Jesus as their Savior and Lord.

Have students write another verse for their class hymn. Today focus on the salvation that Jesus provides for those who trust in, and choose to follow, Him. An example might be:

Jesus, God's Son, was sent to earth

To be the way to God.

If we believe in God's own Son,

We have life eternally.

Have your Juniors stand on their feetographs as they repeat the Unit Verse. Sing the class hymn together. Close with prayer. **We thank you, Jesus, for being willing to die for us in order that we may live for You forever. Amen.**

Follow the Leader ✓

Would-be leaders work hard to get us to follow them. They usually do this by making promises to us. In return, they ask us to make a commitment to do something for them. **In each of the cases below, write a statement you would make to get others to follow you. Use the questions to guide you, but write your statement in your own words.**

Congratulations! You are a candidate for class president! You will have an opportunity to give a campaign speech inviting your classmates to vote for you. What will you say?

If you vote for me, I will_____

_____

_____

In return, I will expect you to_____

_____

_____

You will be glad you did because_____

_____

_____

The long hours of hard work you invested in inventing Brush-O Toothpaste paid off! It's a great new toothpaste that you think everyone should use. Write an advertisement promoting your new product.

If you use Brush-O, it will _____

_____

If you use Brush-O, you will be _____

_____

You will be glad you did because _____

_____

It is the first day of the school year, and you are the teacher of the class. You want everyone to know how much you want them to learn and how good your class can be if you all work together. What will you say to start the year off right?

I am excited to be here because _____

_____

We can have a great year if we _____

_____

You will be glad you did because _____

_____

Jerusalem Investigative Report

ANNOUNCER: Good evening and welcome to the six o'clock news. Tonight we have a special in-depth report from our "I" team about that controversial figure, Jesus of Nazareth. For a background check we call upon our historical reporter, Joseph.

JOSEPH: Little is known about Jesus' life until about three years ago. He has become widely known for the many miracles He has performed. His actions have drawn thousands of curious followers who hope to see more miracles.

ANNOUNCER: Thank you, Joseph. On the political scene, Jesus has recently attracted the attention of the Roman army. For that story we take you to our government correspondent, Quartus.

QUARTUS: The mobs of outcasts that gather around Jesus have made Rome fear a Jewish uprising against Caesar. One of Jesus' close followers is a former member of a radical political group. Even some members of the ruling Jewish religious group, the Sanhedrin, are said to be his followers. Each time Jesus appears the Roman soldiers become very nervous.

ANNOUNCER: Thank you, Quartus. Since you brought up the religious issue, let's hear next from our reporter in the temple. Reuben, you've been on location all day at Solomon's Walkway. What is the feeling of the crowd there?

REUBEN: Things here are very tense tonight. Jesus taught in this very area today and reactions to His message are explosive to say the least. It all began when a group of Jews asked Jesus to tell them who He really was. "If you are the Christ, the one chosen by God to save people from their sins, tell us plainly," they said. In reply Jesus said, and I quote, "I did tell you, but you do not believe. The miracles I do in Father's name speak for me, but you do not believe." Unquote.

He went on to call His followers His sheep and said, "My sheep listen to my voice; I know them, and they follow me. I give them eternal life and they shall never perish. I and My Father are one." At that, the crowd became violent. They picked up stones and prepared to kill Jesus. When He inquired which miracle they were killing him for, they answered that it was not for these good works but because He, only a man, said He was God.

Jesus said that He was the one God chose and sent into the world. He claimed that the miracles He did were the same kinds of things God does and that they prove He is who He says He is. The people tried to grab Jesus, but He escaped.

Opinions differ widely about who Jesus really is, but one thing is certain. No one can remain neutral about Him. His claim to be God's only way to save people from sin forces them to either believe and follow Him or label Him a phony and reject Him.

ANNOUNCER: Thank you, Reuben. And that's the end of our "I" Team Report for tonight. We hope our in-depth investigative study will help you make a decision about Jesus. Good-night.

Lesson 4 ✓

Just Gotta Tell

Aim: That your students will tell others what Jesus has done in their lives.
Scripture: Acts 26:1-23
Unit Verse: I am the way, the truth and the life. No one comes to the Father except through me. John 14:6
Unit Affirmation: I CAN KNOW JESUS PERSONALLY!

✓ Planning Ahead

1. Photocopy activity sheets (pages 119 and 120)–one for each student.
2. Cut 2" circles out of cardboard or Styrofoam meat trays, two for each student. Cut 3" squares of clear contact paper, four for each student. Make samples of the shoe ties according to the directions in SETTING THE STAGE.
3. Copy the student written hymn verse from last week onto the class hymn poster board.

1 Setting the Stage (5-10 minutes)

WHAT YOU'LL DO

• Make shoe ties that tell the Good News of God's love for us

WHAT YOU'LL NEED

• Cardboard circles, clear contact paper squares, paper punch, drawing supplies

2 Introducing the Issue (20 minutes)

WHAT YOU'LL DO

• Participate in a Good News circle to illustrate the many ways we talk about good news in our lives
• Use an activity sheet to outline the Good News about Jesus we can share with others
• Complete the Unit Affirmation poster

WHAT YOU'LL NEED

• "GOOD NEWS!" Activity Sheet (page 119)
• Unit Affirmation poster

3 Searching the Scriptures (20 minutes)

WHAT YOU'LL DO

• Use an activity sheet and read a Bible-times newspaper to understand that telling others about Jesus involves telling what Jesus has done in their lives
• Observe an object lesson to see how Jesus helps us witness for Him

WHAT YOU'LL NEED

• Bibles
• "Caesarea Scribe" Activity Sheet (page 120)
• Dime, plastic drinking straw, small glass of water

4 Living the Lesson (5-10 minutes)

WHAT YOU'LL DO

• Think about something that Jesus has done and tell another person about it
• Write a verse for the class hymn focusing on the salvation that Jesus provides for those who trust in, and choose to follow, Him

WHAT YOU'LL NEED

• Copies of "O For A Thousand Tongues To Sing," syllable accent chart from "Who Is Jesus?" Lesson One, poster board copy of class hymn
• Optional: Rhyming dictionary, thesaurus

113

✔ Setting the Stage (5-10 minutes)

As your students arrive today give each Junior two 2" cardboard circles (See PLANNING AHEAD.) and four 3" squares of clear contact paper. Instruct them

to decorate the circles to create shoe ties that tell the Good News about Jesus' love for us. If you have made a sample, display it to give the kids the idea. When their design is complete, they will cover the circles with the clear contact paper and punch two holes in the top of each. They can now be threaded onto their shoe laces and worn as a witness to God's love in Jesus.

Why do we say that Jesus' love for us is Good News? When we find things in our lives that are good news, the first thing we want to do is find someone to tell! Today we will talk about how telling others the good news about Jesus' love is a special part of knowing Him personally.

✔ Introducing the Issue (20 minutes)

Whenever something good happens in our lives we usually find a way to tell someone about it. Have you ever had something happen that you were so excited about you thought you would burst if you didn't tell someone right away? Let kids share examples of times they have felt this way. You may want to begin by sharing an example from your own life. There are lots of things that happen in our lives that we want to tell others about. **What kinds of things do we want to tell?** Lead the discussion to include these categories: things we did or experienced (played in a recital; went to Disneyland; no cavities at the dentist); good news about someone else (Mary got over the mumps and came back to school; Jason was elected class president); things that will help others solve a problem or enjoy life more (if you tell Mr. Jamison he'll let you choose a different book to report on; I think you'd really like playing on our basketball team. Come with me next week!) **What are some ways we can tell good news to others?** Encourage kids to think creatively about this question. Make a list of items on the board as they think of things. The obvious answers are sharing face to face, call on the telephone, or write a note or letter. Wearing shoe ties, leaving a picture on the refrigerator, or doing handsprings can also communicate a message. On the extreme side, we could rent a billboard, hire a skywriter, or wear a sandwich board!

If your class is not already sitting in a circle, seat them in one now. **Let's have some fun by participating in a Good News Circle. We will see how long we can think of good news items to share with each other. These can be real things or made up things. The idea is to see just how much good news we talk about everyday!** Say it like this: The good news is _____, and I want to tell others by _____. For example, "The good news is I got an A on my geography test and I want to tell everyone by making an announcement over the school P.A. system! Now ask for a volunteer to start and then proceed around the circle. Keep going for as long as the kids think of good news items to share. Remember, these can be about personal experiences or accomplishments, news about others, or news about things that will make our lives better (Brush-O toothpaste is the best toothpaste I ever tasted!). This is meant to be a light, fun activity that the whole class can enjoy.

Distribute copies of the activity sheet, "GOOD NEWS!" (page 119). **The Bible says that we are to tell others the GOOD NEWS about Jesus. What is there about Jesus that's good news?** As kids suggest things, have them write them on the lines on the activity sheet. Guide the conversation to include these things:

He loves me. The fact that Jesus came to earth is a sign of His love for us.

He forgives my sins. To know God, who is perfect or sinless, means we have to get rid of our sins. Jesus' death on the cross does that.

He gives me eternal life. Jesus' love extends beyond death and gives us a home in heaven.

He answers my prayers. Jesus is present with us through prayer all through our lives.

He teaches me how to live. Through the Bible, we learn Jesus' way of living is the best!

He gives me a new family. The church family is a significant resource for living our lives.

When you look at all those things together, it is easy to see that knowing Jesus is not only Good News, it is the most important good news we could ever tell someone! Thinking back on all the ways we found to tell

our good news to others, how many of those ways could we use to tell others about Jesus? Let kids review the list on the board and think of ways they could apply those methods of sharing good news to telling others about Jesus.

Display the Unit Affirmation poster and have the class read the Affirmation aloud. Since this is the last week of the unit, review the three phrases and what they tell us about knowing Jesus personally. Then write, "And invite others to know Him, too!" on the last line. **Although knowing Jesus personally is good news, sometimes it is not the easiest Good News to share with others. Let's look in on one of Paul's experiences and see what we can learn about sharing the Good News about Jesus with others.**

 # Searching the Scriptures (20 minutes)

Distribute copies of the activity sheet "Caesarea Scribe" (page 120). **When Paul lived there were no printed newspapers like we have today, but if there had been this is what one might have been like. Let's see how eager the Apostle Paul was to tell others about the good things that had happened to Him since He decided to follow Jesus.** Ask several students to read the articles aloud.

Ask a volunteer to look up Acts 26:9-11 and read it aloud. **What had Paul been doing before he chose to follow Jesus?** (Persecuting Christians, putting the followers of Jesus in jail and killing them.) Have someone check out Acts 26:16 and read it aloud. **Why did Jesus appear to Paul?** (To appoint him to be a servant and witness to Jesus, tell everyone what Jesus had done for him.) **What is a witness?** (Someone who tells what she or he heard, saw, or knows.)

What method did Paul use to witness for Jesus? (He told others what Jesus had done for him, told others that Jesus had died for them and was the Savior of all people.) Guide your students to understand that "witnessing" is basically telling others what Jesus has done for them. They don't need to learn a lot of theology or memorize all the Gospels in order to share Jesus with others. They are witnesses by simply telling how He loves and cares for them.

Have someone read aloud Acts 26:2. **How did Paul feel about being a prisoner on trial for telling others about Jesus?** (He was fortunate, happy to do it.) Paul didn't complain about his imprisonment and its hardships. Instead, he saw every trouble as another opportunity to tell people about Jesus. Paul was more concerned about helping others know about the salvation Jesus offered than he was about his own problems. **How do we often feel if difficulties arise when we are trying to tell others about Jesus?**

(Sad, angry, afraid, ashamed, discouraged.)

Sometimes we are afraid or feel we don't know enough to be able to share our faith with others. Lay a dime and a plastic drinking straw on the table. Call someone to the table. (Name of student) **I want you to put one end of the straw on this dime and pick it up by sucking on the straw.** Have kid try this. She or he will be unable to do so. Explain that the inability to perform this feat is an illustration of how helpless we often feel about sharing Jesus with others.

Set out the glass of water and instruct the student to dip one end of the straw into it. **We'll let the water represent the loving aid that God gives when we ask Him to help us witness for Jesus.** Have the student try to lift the coin again, this time placing the wet end of the straw on the dime. Encourage him or her to suck in hard. The dime can now be lifted high. **When we combine God's power with our weakness we can do things we thought were impossible.**

What do you think we can learn from Paul's example in today's story? (We can take advantage of our problems, use them as chances to share Jesus with others.) Help your students regard their problems as opportunities to tell people who might not be reached otherwise. In many areas of the world today Christians face great difficulties as they share their faith. Encourage your kids to be partners with these brothers and sisters in Christ by praying for them and becoming informed World Christians.

In the Bible-time newspaper how did Festus react to Paul's message? (Called him crazy.) **Not everyone responds gladly when we tell them of what Jesus has done for us, but that can't stop the joy of God from blessing our own lives.** Have someone look up II Corinthians 7:4-7 and read it aloud. **How did Paul feel about the people who chose to follow Jesus after he had witnessed to them?** (Happy, proud of them, encouraged by them, joyful.) **Point out that Paul felt the results of helping others follow Jesus was worth more than any troubles he had gone through to share Christ with them.**

Living the Lesson (5-10 minutes)

Discuss the mechanics of sharing Jesus with others. This will help prepare your Juniors to witness to others. Guide them to think about the following questions: **When are some times that we might have opportunities to tell someone about what Jesus has done for us? How do you start? What do you say? What do you do if they don't want to listen to you?**

Focus on sharing out of love and concern for others. Down play any preach-

ing at or condemning of the listener. Encourage kids to take advantage of the curiosity of others about the differences in life-styles of Christians. Point out that they can't assume someone doesn't want to know about God. Stress the importance of prayer and the leading of the Holy Spirit as they reach out to friends and family.

When Jesus becomes our best friend and loving Savior, it is such good news that we want to tell others about what He has done for us. What has Jesus done for you? Have students take a few minutes to think about this question. At this point they are only to think about it, not say anything. Divide the class into pairs. Each partner will briefly tell the other something that Jesus has done for him or her. Encourage them to make this something recent, not from a long time ago.

Have students look up John 14:6 and say it together. **What do you think Jesus meant when He said He was the life?** (Students will probably focus on eternal or everlasting life.) Enlarge their vision to see that the life Jesus is talking about is more than that.

Ask someone to look up John 10:10b and read it aloud. **What kind of life did Jesus come to bring those who follow Him?** (Full.) **What is a "full" life?** Help your Juniors realize that this means more than a long life or one that is full of earthly pleasures, riches, and fame. These things are only temporary. Only by following Jesus can we know what a truly satisfying life is and have eternal, everlasting life as well. **The kind of full life that Jesus brings is what we want to tell others about.**

Display the syllable accent chart and class hymn poster. Complete the hymn by writing a verse that focuses on witnessing to others about Jesus. Sing all the verses of this original song. Sending homes individual copies of the song will reinforce the truths learned in this unit.

Have students silently pray for someone with whom they would like to share Jesus. Close by asking God to help them have an opportunity to witness to these people soon.

He_____
_____
_____
_____

He_____
_____
_____

I Can Know Jesus Personally and That's Good News!

He_____
_____
_____
_____
_____

He_____
_____
_____
_____

He_____
_____
_____
_____

He_____
_____
_____
_____

Caesarea Scribe

Caesarea, Samaria   Tuesday, July 19, 60 A.D.   5 shekels

Paul On Trial!

Official Claims Prisoner Insane

Caesarea—The famed Apostle of Christianity, Paul, appeared in court today before the Roman governor, Porcius Festus, the Jewish King Agrippa, and Queen Bernice. Although Paul is a prisoner and waiting to be sent on to Caesar for a court trial, he was allowed to tell government officials about his relationship with Jesus, also called God's Son.

Paul the Apostle

Governor Festus

Upset by Paul's speech today, Governor Festus called him insane. The prisoner denied this and in a surprise move urged King Agrippa to follow Jesus as he himself does.

PUBLIC OPINION POLL

Today's question: "What do you think about telling others about Jesus?"

Peter: You should always be ready to answer people who ask you about your hope in Jesus.

Rachel: It is a good idea.

Thomas: I doubt if people would listen to me. But if they did I'd say He's my Lord and my God!

Prisoner Tells His Story

Paul, the prisoner begged his audience to listen to him patiently as he told them about his earlier life of following strict religious rules and opposing the name of Jesus of Nazareth.

He went on to recount a period of persecution when he personally put many followers of Jesus in prison and voted for their deaths. "I even went to foreign cities to persecute them," Paul declared sadly.

His mood changed to joy as he told how he became a follower of Jesus. As he was on his way to Damascus to persecute the Christians there, he was struck down by a bright light and heard a voice.

"I heard a voice call me by name. It asked me why I persecuted him. I asked, Who are you Lord? He said, 'I am Jesus...I have appointed you as a servant and a witness of what you have seen of me. I am sending you to turn people from darkness to light and from Satan to God, so they may receive forgiveness of sins and a place among those who are sanctified by faith in me,'" the prisoner stated.

Paul told King Agrippa that he had been obedient to that call from Jesus and is telling everyone that because Jesus had been sinless, died and lives again He is the Savior who saves people from sin and restores them to a personal relationship with God.

Service Projects for Who is Jesus?

✔ 1. Create tracts giving personal testimonies. These could be given to someone with whom you want to share Jesus.

✔ 2. Design a "Sharing Time" program using puppets, mime, clowns, musical instruments, brief spoken testimonies or songs that speak of what it means to know Jesus. Present the program at church, school, in nursing homes, retirement centers, or Bible camps.

✔ 3. Develop an in-depth training program that will teach other kids how to share Jesus in informal ways.

✔ 4. Start a "Kids, INC." (In Christ) Club personal outreach ministry using a theme such as Pen Pals; Big/Little Sisters/Brothers; Adopt a Grandparent; Friends to Shut-Ins, Handicapped, Nursing Home Residents; Baby-Sitting Club; Migrant or Homeless Pals.

✔ 5. Have a work project to do a variety of tasks. You can: help at inner-city or urban playgrounds, gather and distribute used clothes or toys, help elderly with home maintenance chores, work at a food shelf or homeless shelter, do odd-jobs or janitorial tasks at a church; help at a Vacation Bible School.

Just Add Kids

Quick Bible Lessons to Pick Up 'N Do!

Get the first two volumes hot off the press in April 2004!

This all new resource is cost-effective and totally class-efficient! An entire quarter of Sunday School (twelve lessons) in one book! This economical new concept in elementary curricula gives your kids in-depth Bible teaching and serious discipleship without hours of preparation or lots of staff. Here's why you and your kids will love *Just Add Kids*:

• **Instant fun-filled dramas take a unique approach to the Bible stories.**
• **Engages knowledgeable students while giving kids who are new to God's Word a solid foundation of Biblical truth.**
• **Perfect for the ministry with large group sessions and small group shepherding time!**
• **Copy "n" go handouts bring the lessons to life.**
• **Optional hands-on workshops stretch each lesson with a craft, science or food activity.**

Jesus 4U!
Item#: 103326 ISBN: 0-78144-069-6

Take Two Tablets and Call Moses
Item#:103324   ISBN: 0-78144-067-X

128 pages; 8.5 x 11; $19.99 *(Canada $29.99)*

Bible Fun Stuff

Excellent Resources for Children & Teachers!

Collect all 13 books in the series!

Children's ministry can be fun and meaningful when you use these incredible creative resources from Godprints. Every activity comes with a Godprint, Bible Truth and Bible Verse to help kids learn what God is like and how to become more like Him! 8.5 x 11, $16.99 each *(Canada $24.99)*

NEW! Down in Front Children's Sermons

Take kids on exciting adventures through Bible times where they'll discover that Bible places were real towns full of real people.
ISBN: 0-78144-083-1 ITEM #: 103452 112P

NEW! Fun Science That Teaches God's Word

60 activities that reflect God's incredible creation in science are arranged in four categories.
ISBN: 0-78144-081-5 ITEM #: 103450 112P

NEW! Toddlerific

Faith building activities for Toddlers and twos. Includes reproducibles for creating Bible story "books" children can safely handle.
ISBN: 0-78144-082-3 ITEM #: 103451 112P

Children's Sermons In a Bag
ISBN: 0-78143-958-2 ITEM #: 102361 112P

Every Season Kid Pleasin' Children's Sermons
ISBN: 0-78143-839-X ITEM #: 101780 112P

FUNtastic Kid Crafts
ISBN: 0-78143-838-1 ITEM #: 101777 112P

Paper Capers
ISBN: 0-78143-836-5 ITEM #: 101778 112P

A Gaggle of Giggles and Games
ISBN: 0-78143-840-3 ITEM #: 101781 112P

Folder Games for Children's Ministry
ISBN: 0-78143-961-2
ITEM #: 102364 140P

The Official Puppet Ministry Survival Guide
ISBN: 0-78143-841-1
ITEM #: 101782 112P

Seasonal Pageants and Skits
ISBN: 0-78143-959-0
ITEM #: 102362 112P

Teaching Off the Wall: Interactive Bulletin Boards
ISBN: 0-78143-837-3 ITEM #: 101779 112P

Wiggle Worms Learn the Psalms
ISBN: 0-78143-960-4 ITEM #: 102363 112P

Creative Bible
Activities for Children

100's of Songs, Games and More!

Bring the Bible to life and help your kids stay interested in learning with these fun activities, songs and crafts! Over 1200 action-packed ideas at your fingertips. $16.99 (Can. $24.99)

Preschoolers
ISBN: 0-78143-966-3 ITEM #: 102859
8.5 x 11, 157p

School Kids
ISBN: 0-78143-965-5 ITEM #: 102858
8.5 x 11, 143p

One Rehearsal Christmas Plays
$12.99   ISBN 0-78144-120-X
ITEM #: 103618 8.5 x 11, 96p

Bible Memory Games
$16.99 (Can. $24.99) ISBN 0-78144-119-6
ITEM #: 103617 8.5 x 11, 143p

Spur-of-the-Moment Crafts
$12.99; ISBN 0-78144-121-8; ITEM #: 103619

Spur-of-the-Moment Games
$12.99; ISBN 0-78144-118-8; ITEM #: 103616

Life and Lessons of Jesus Series
(4-Volume Series)

Make Jesus real for kids with reproducible, easy-to-do and fun activities! Each volume is packed with dozens of projects that you won't find anywhere else!

$24.99 each (Can. $37.99), 8 1/2 x 11, PB

Vol 1—Jesus' Early Years
ISBN: 0-78143-847-0
ITEM #: 101841

Vol 2—Jesus' Ministry
ISBN: 0-78143-848-9
ITEM #: 101842

Vol 3—Following Jesus
ISBN: 0-78143-849-7
ITEM #: 101843

Vol 4—The Love of Jesus
ISBN: 0-78143-850-0
ITEM #: 101844

The Word at Work . . . Around the World

hat would you do if you wanted to share God's love with children on the streets of your city? That's the dilemma David C. Cook faced in 1870s Chicago. His answer was to create literature that would capture children's hearts.

Out of those humble beginnings grew a worldwide ministry that has used literature to proclaim God's love and disciple generation after generation. Cook Communications Ministries is committed to personal discipleship—to helping people of all ages learn God's Word, embrace his salvation, walk in his ways, and minister in his name.

Opportunities—and Crisis

We live in a land of plenty—including plenty of Christian literature! But what about the rest of the world? Jesus commanded, "Go and make disciples of all nations" (Matt. 28:19) and we want to obey this commandment. But how does a publishing organization "go" into all the world?

There are five times as many Christians around the world as there are in North America. Christian workers in many of these countries have no more than a New Testament, or perhaps a single shared copy of the Bible, from which to learn and teach.

We are committed to sharing what God has given us with such Christians.

A vital part of Cook Communications Ministries is our international outreach, Cook Communications Ministries International (CCMI). Your purchase of this book, and of other books and Christian-growth products from Cook, enables CCMI to provide Bibles and Christian literature to people in more than 150 languages in 65 countries.

Cook Communications Ministries is a not-for-profit, self-supporting organization. Revenues from sales of our books, Bible curriculum, and other church and home products not only fund our U.S. ministry, but also fund our CCMI ministry around the world. One hundred percent of donations to CCMI go to our international literature programs.

CCMI reaches out internationally in three ways:

• Our premier International Christian Publishing Institute (ICPI) trains leaders from nationally led publishing houses around the world to develop evangelism and discipleship materials to transform lives in their countries.

• We provide literature for pastors, evangelists, and Christian workers in their national language. We provide study helps for pastors and lay leaders in many parts of the world, such as China, India, Cuba, Iran, and Vietnam.

• We reach people at risk—refugees, AIDS victims, street children, and famine victims—with God's Word. CCMI puts literature that shares the Good News into the hands of people at spiritual risk—people who might die before they hear the name of Jesus and are transformed by his love.

Word Power—God's Power

Faith Kidz, RiverOak, Honor, Life Journey, Victor, NexGen — every time you purchase a book produced by Cook Communications Ministries, you not only meet a vital personal need in your life or in the life of someone you love, but you're also a part of ministering to José in Colombia, Humberto in Chile, Gousa in India, or Lidiane in Brazil. You help make it possible for a pastor in China, a child in Peru, or a mother in West Africa to enjoy a life-changing book. And because you helped, children and adults around the world are learning God's Word and walking in his ways.

Thank you for your partnership in helping to disciple the world. May God bless you with the power of his Word in your life.

For more information about our international ministries, visit www.ccmi.org.